RAINS
all the
TIME

RAINS
all the
TIME

A Connoisseur's
History of Weather
in the Pacific Northwest

DAVID LASKIN

SASQUATCH BOOKS
SEATTLE

Printed in the United States of America.
Distributed in Canada by Raincoast Books Ltd.
01 00 99 98 97   5 4 3 2 1

Cover design: Karen Schober
Cover photograph: Alan Berner/ *Seattle Times*
Interior design and composition: Kate Basart

Library of Congress Cataloging in Publication Data
Laskin, David, 1953–
        Rains all the time : a connoisseur's history of weather in the Pacific
Northwest / David Laskin.
                        p.   cm.
        Includes bibliographical references and index.
    Select Bibliography
        ISBN 1-57061-063-0
        1. Northwest, Pacific—Climate. 2. Rain and rainfall—Northwest, Pacific.
I. Title.
        QC984.N97L37 1997
        5551.69795—dc21   97-16051

SASQUATCH BOOKS
615 Second Avenue
Seattle, Washington 98104
(206) 467-4300
books@sasquatchbooks.com
http://www.sasquatchbooks.com

Sasquatch Books publishes high-quality adult nonfiction and children's books related
to the Northwest (Alaska to San Francisco). For more information about our titles,
contact us at the address above, or view our site on the World Wide Web.

CONTENTS

To Fergus

who was wonderfully suited to our weather

ACKNOWLEDGMENTS

I could not have written this book without the help I received from Northwest meteorologists, climatologists, climate researchers, and weather buffs. I am especially grateful to Brad Colman of the Seattle National Weather Service forecast office for patience and generosity beyond the call of duty. I would also like to thank Clifford Mass and John M. Wallace of the University of Washington department of atmospheric sciences; Nick Bond, who holds a joint appointment with the National Oceanic and Atmospheric Administration's Pacific Marine Environmental Lab and the University of Washington's Joint Institute for the Study of the Atmosphere and Ocean; Nathan Mantua with the Joint Institute for the Study of the Atmosphere and Ocean; Jack Capell of KGW-TV in Portland; Steve Todd and Dave Willson of the Portland National Weather Service forecast office; George Miller, recently retired from the Portland forecast office; Mark Albright, the state climatologist for Washington; and George Taylor, Oregon's state climatologist.

My research was facilitated by the staffs of the Suzzallo Library Special Collections at the University of Washington and the Oregon History Center in Portland. I'd like to thank Carla Rickerson at the Suzzallo Special Collections for advice and a useful reading list.

In Chapter Three and in the section on winter, I drew extensively on Steve Mierzejewski's unpublished manuscript *Footprints on the Rivers,* a rich source of information and weather quotations from early explorers, settlers, and journalists in the Pacific Northwest. Mierzejewski did a masterful job of combing through archives with an eye to reconstructing the weather of times past. His manuscript, available at the Oregon History Center in Portland, deserves to be published. I also found Robert A. Bennett's *We'll All Go Home in the Spring: Personal Accounts and Adventures As Told By the Pioneers of the West* extremely helpful for the letters, diaries, and impressions it gathered.

Many friends and acquaintances shared their local weather lore (often unwittingly) and put up with my endless questions about their memories of seasons past. Thank you Jane and Roger Lowell, Nils and Synnove Dragoy, Jim and Rita Vincent, Cindy Esselman, Janis Mercker, Jane Ellis, Jack Litweka, Skip Berger, and David Brewster.

I'm grateful to my editor, Gary Luke, for his enthusiasm about this project and for his thoughtful edit of the manuscript. My agent, Diane Cleaver, was always keen on weather writing, and she undertook this project with her customary grace and zeal. Diane died before the book's contract was finished—all who knew her miss her still. I want to thank Heide Lange for picking up where Diane left off and for her support and warmth in the past few years.

Finally, a big hug to my family—my wife, Kate O'Neill, and our three daughters, Emily, Sarah, and Alice—for putting up with me through yet another weather book. They know, better than anyone, just how obsessed with rain I can be.

Chapter One

*"A climate
where being
is bliss"*

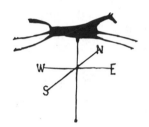

AN INTRODUCTION TO NORTHWEST WEATHER

I T IS THE FIRST WORD OUT OF THE mouths of arriving visitors. It is the symbol and mascot of the region. A joke. A myth. The inspiration of poems and shimmering prose effusions and muttered curses. The trigger of countless cases of depression. As precious as gold. As common as dirt. Hard to predict. Impossible to summon, control, or stop.

Rain. No matter that Seattle and Portland receive less of it on average than New York City or Washington, D.C. No matter that much of the territory east of the Cascades is starved for it. No matter that it usually nearly ceases almost everywhere in the region for two and sometimes three months a year. No matter. Rain is indelibly imprinted on the climatic reputation of the Pacific Northwest. "We . . . tend to think we have some sort of proprietary claim to rain," a local newspaper columnist wrote recently. "It's our defining characteristic, responsible for everything from our clothing—layered—to our temperament—boring." We're stuck with it and have been for as far back as our history goes (which, of course, isn't very far; Native Americans unfortunately kept no written records of their interpretations of the climate). "It is called rainy," David Blaine, Seattle's first Methodist minister, wrote to his parents on January 24, 1855, when the "city of Seattle" was all of four years old, "but it very seldom rains more than a few hours at a time, and then we have fair weather for a few days, but rainy nights. . . ." Blaine should have saved his ink and paper. It was called rainy then and it would be called rainy again, no matter how many settlers and visitors and sightseers raved in letters "back home" about the region's genial, healthful, invigorating conditions.

Half a century after Blaine, newspaperman Charles Prosch, a New Yorker who migrated to San Francisco in 1857 and then relocated blissfully to the southern end of Puget Sound, wrote in his *Reminiscences of Washington Territory* (1904): "Much ignorance, not unmingled with some prejudice and incredulity, existed abroad for many years in regard to the climate of Washington. And this notwithstanding the earnest efforts of the first settlers and the pioneer press to enlighten the outside world. But it would not be enlightened, for the reason that many intelligent Eastern people obstinately persisted in thinking that it ought, and therefore must rain, hail, snow and freeze here nine months in the year; such weather being the natural sequence of its high northern latitude. In vain were they assured of the contrary; it could not be other that they thought and believed."

So it was in 1904. So it is today. And so it ever shall be. It is not just obstinate Easterners who refuse to be enlightened: lots of natives and longtime residents who should know better have perpetuated the myth of incessant rain, as I discovered in the course of working on this book about what people have written, thought, said, believed, and imagined about our weather over the past 400 years. It has been very wet reading. "It was raining, of course," historian Murray Morgan began a section of *The Last Wilderness,* his 1955 history of the Olympic Peninsula. "It was not quite raining, but everything was wet," wrote Annie Dillard of a typical October day in western Washington. "O! how horriable is the day," William Clark wept in soggy misspelled frustration on the Oregon coast as yet another rainstorm pounded down on him and Meriwether Lewis and the members of their Corps of Discovery during the winter of 1805–6. Scottish explorer David Douglas (for whom the Douglas fir is named), though usually more tolerant of wet weather than Lewis and Clark, bemoaned being caught out in a classic Northwest camping disaster near the Umpqua River in October 1826: "The rain, driven by the violence of the wind, rendered it impossible for me to keep any fire, and to add misery to my affliction my tent was blown down at midnight." "Rain poured down in torrents the whole day," sniffed the artist Paul Kane, describing his attempt to travel to Nisqually, at the southern end of Puget Sound, in April 1858. "The mud is so very deep in this pass that we were compelled to dismount and drag our horses through it by the bridles, the poor beasts being up to their bellies in mud of the tenacity of bird-lime." Even when the rain lets up for a moment, the sky usually remains angry and ominous. As novelist Tom Robbins wrote of yet another dull autumnal dawn over the Skagit Valley: "The day was rumpled and dreary. It looked like Edgar Allan Poe's pajamas."

One advantage of a really bad climatic reputation is that newcomers and visitors are often surprised that the weather isn't *worse*. There is a whole subgenre of amazed accounts of Northwest days, weeks, even seasons turning out far better than expected—mild, frost-free winters; warm rainless summers; glorious early springs. Novelist Bernard Malamud, a native of New York who taught in western Oregon for nearly a decade, studded his 1961 novel *A New Life* with such meteorological amazement, as in this musing on the unexpected pleasures of the blurry Northwest seasons: "At times the clouds massed darkly, yet the day managed to be cheery, and the bright green winter wheat yielded hidden light. Levin [the novel's hero] guessed the temperature was around fifty, and this they called onset of winter. . . . Who immersed in Eastern snow and icy winds could guess at Cascadia's pleasant weather? Here . . . spring came sometimes in midwinter; autumn in the right mood might hang on till January, and at times spring lingered through summer."

Being a relative newcomer myself, I know this sense of seasonal dislocation and meteorological bewilderment. When we arrived in Seattle, in the middle of July 1993, it was raining (of course) and chilly—a high of only 59 degrees Fahrenheit* on July 20 (this they called summer?). We did eventually have a summer that year, only it started late—on August 4 the temperature hit 95° (this they called mild?) and by September we were having an unbroken spell of gloriously warm clear days. Total rainfall in Seattle that September was .03 inch—barely enough rain to smudge the dirt on my car. New York's Central Park, by contrast,

All temperatures in this book are in Fahrenheit.

received 5.25 inches of rain that month. I was beginning to wonder about this legendary Northwest rain—but of course natives and longtime residents were laughing up their sleeves. "Just wait," they kept telling me. "Just wait." I later learned that all of this— my startled reaction to regional precipitation patterns, and the local reaction to my reaction—was part of the standard baptism into the mysteries of Northwest weather. There is even an evolving sub-sub-genre of natives issuing dire (and exaggerated) climatic warnings to scare off would-be new settlers. Boris Biancheri, Italy's ambassador to the United States, cannily recognized this in an essay about his summer vacation in the Pacific Northwest: "The local rain god must have been distracted as I passed through, because in weeks I never saw more than five or six clouds, and even they were candid, light, innocent. . . . Perhaps those who live here paint the climate as more hostile than it is, partly because of the pleasure insiders take in describing to outsiders what is unique and different in their environment and partly because of a secret desire to discourage potential residents."

So we've come full circle: from pioneers in the 1840s and 1850s earnestly trying (and failing) to persuade the folks back East that the Northwest has "the most equable and healthful climate on the globe" to their descendants in the 1990s earnestly insisting that the rumors are true—it's every bit as bad as you always heard it was. And then some.

The reality of our climate is surprising enough. Even more surprising is how many different climates exist in the region. In a few hours you can drive from coastal rain forests, where towering hemlocks and cedars soak up an average of 150 inches of rainfall a year, to sagebrush deserts that are lucky to eke out 10 inches of precipitation in twelve months. Climatic transitions are sometimes gradual—as around Puget Sound, where rainfall diminishes inch by inch as you move north from Olympia to Everett and increases as you ascend the Cascade foothills—and sometimes stunningly abrupt. The region's most dramatic transition is between the windward and leeward sides of Washington's Olympic Mountains: slopes facing the Pacific can receive as much as 250 inches of rain annually, while at the town of Sequim, about fifty miles behind the mountain barrier, a mere 16 inches accumulates in an average year—less than Los Angeles normally gets. What happens in places like Sequim is the work of that wonderfully named phenomenon "the rain shadow." When moist Pacific air hits the mountains it is forced to rise, and as it rises it cools; the cooling causes the water vapor to condense and fall as rain. Lots and lots of rain. Hence the rain forests where, as one writer puts it, trees grow so tall that "the murmur of the wind in the branches is indistinct, and the rays of the midday sun filter down like light into deep water." Once the wrung-out Pacific air masses cross the mountain crests and start to descend, they warm up slightly and the clouds scatter. Sun peeks through. Earth remains dry. Rain shadow.

The Olympic rain shadow is relatively small, encompassing the northern section of the Olympic Peninsula and to a lesser extent the San Juan Islands, a band of Whidbey Island, and southern Vancouver Island. But the Cascade rain shadow is enormous, effectively slicing Washington and Oregon into two radically different climatic zones. The divide is stark and startling and surreal. The first time we drove east over the North Cascades Highway, I caught a catnap while my wife took the wheel; my eyes closed on Switzerland and blinked open on Arizona. Oregon writer Sallie Tisdale wrote of this sharp climatic divide in her lovely Northwest history-memoir-meditation *Stepping Westward:*

> At every pass up and down the length of the Cascades,
> on every ridge where the pines stand up like bristles
> of a toothbrush, is a border: The soil changes, the
> trees and rocks change, the sky and the temperature
> and the light change. The transition is both reliable
> and abrupt. Sagebrush and scattered ponderosa
> replace hemlock and vine maple; tules and cattails
> replace ferns. Most of Oregon and Washington lies
> east of the Cascade spine, where the fall color arrives
> first. In the space of a half-mile, you can go from
> summer green to autumn gold.

It's a fact we usually forget: geographically, most of the Pacific Northwest is actually arid or semiarid. Stewart Holbrook, a prominent Northwest journalist from the late 1930s until his death in 1964, noted that the north-to-south-running Cascade crest makes a lot more sense as a regional dividing line than the east-to-west-running Columbia River, which forms much of the Washington-Oregon border. As Holbrook wrote in his book *Northwest Corner,* the mountains give the two sections "disparate climates":

> On the west, rain is something that comes without
> prayers—making the beaver with his webbed feet a
> symbol for those of us west of the mountains. On the
> east, a few drops of moisture are often occasion for a
> front-page story in the local papers. Equable tempera-

tures, with little and sometimes no annual snows, are
found on the west. On the east, snow comes down
generously and the mercury often hits forty and more
degrees below zero. Complexions on the east side are
said to be two shades darker, by reason of sun and
wind, than on the west. . . .

Oregon and Washington men and women from east
of the range are said to come from the cow counties,
or the wheat counties. Their thoughts, and their votes,
are as likely to be connected with irrigation as anything else.

While folks in Portland and Seattle joke, and get teased, about
the ceaseless precipitation (we don't tan, we rust; when the sun
finally does come out in July, we get a prune tan), east of the
mountains they have their own dry wit. "We measure humidity by
the amount of sand in the air," wrote E. R. Jackman and R. A.
Long in their book *The Oregon Desert*. "When it rains, we keep our
hired man in—we want all the water on the land. . . . The kind
of storm we pray for is a couple of feet of wet snow, a foot of
manure on top, then a boiling hot rain. We haven't had it yet." On
a more serious note, Jackman and Long pointed out that a full
quarter of Oregon—24,000 square miles, or roughly the area of
West Virginia—is desert: "It is rough, petrified grandeur. It is
dry, cold, hot, sandy, and full of geology. An awful lot of wind
passes through."

The mountains that obstruct the westward passage of rain and
clouds also block the eastward movement of continental air
masses, which tend to be torrid in the summer and frigid in
winter. As Walter Rue remarked in his *Weather of the Pacific Coast:*
"How different our climate would be if our western mountains

(the main ranges) ran east-west instead of north-south, with Portland, Seattle, Vancouver, and Victoria on the north side of those ranges. We would then have fierce winters every year."

The Cascades split the Northwest into moist maritime west and dry continental east—our two major climatic zones. But within each zone, microclimates abound. The mountains themselves host a rainbow of climates, a distinct band of temperature and precipitation emerging with every few thousand feet of elevation. An ascent up Mount Rainier takes you through four distinct climatic zones, starting at the base with the humid transition zone of gigantic firs, hemlocks, and cedars, and ending 14,410 feet above sea level at the arctic-alpine summit. Our glacier- and river-carved valleys, saltwater sounds and straits, lakes, and intermittent lowlands also do strange things to the weather. The varied terrain riddles the atmosphere with roadblocks and funnels, chutes and channels that warp, fold, wring, and squeeze the air masses. Ice storms bred in the Columbia Gorge encase Portland in treacherous crystal while nearby Oregon City stays warm and dry; convergence zones distribute rainfall as unevenly as wealth around Puget Sound; winds suddenly shift direction when they hit the San Juan Islands; snow that buries the Kitsap Peninsula barely grazes adjacent Bainbridge Island. At any given hour it might be pouring in Everett, sunny in downtown Seattle, overcast at Sea-Tac airport, drizzling on Portland, blowing hard on Astoria, dead calm in Medford, and snowing on Mount Rainier.

So there is a lot more variety and complexity out here than is commonly supposed. It doesn't rain all the time after all. In much of the region it barely rains at all. And even when it does rain, it rarely storms hard enough to erode your yard or knock down your house. The Northwest is far less prone to meteorological catastrophes than most other sections of the country. As University of Washington atmospheric scientist Phil Church wrote in 1962, the year Seattle hosted the World's Fair: "We residents of Western Washington are thankful to be cheated from witnessing or being subjected to nearly all the vicious display of huge atmospheric energy bursts such as hurricanes, tornadoes, severe thunderstorms, dust storms, cloudbursts, blizzards, ice storms, cold and hot waves that people in other sections of the country must endure."

But let's not go overboard. This is not Provence, Tahiti, or southern California. Western Washington and Oregon do, after all, get wet an average of 150 days each year. It may be just a little drizzle or a passing shower or a heavy mist: anything over .01 inch gets counted as rain, and we get it nearly half the days in the year. But only in certain months. That's the other significant fact about rainfall in our region: it's bunched up in one end of the year. Nearly half of the year's total rain comes down in just three months—November, December, and January. Tack on October and February and you get a five-month rainy season that accounts for about 65 percent of the yearly rainfall. It's been known to rain for five weeks straight in the winter; on the other hand, droughts lasting thirty or more consecutive days are common in summer. In the summer of 1967, Portland had seventy-one dry days in a row and Seattle had seventy, with rainfall for July and August *combined* measuring .03 inch; no rain fell on Seattle for forty-eight consecutive days in the summer of 1922. Explorer and naturalist John Muir, journeying up from California toward the end of the nineteenth century, painted this miniature sketch of the wet and dry times of year in western Oregon: "The climate . . . is rather damp and sloppy throughout the winter months, but the summers are bright, ripening the wheat and allowing it to be garnered in good condition. Taken as a whole, the weather is bland and kindly, and like the forest trees the crops and cattle grow plump and sound in it." The alternation of rainy and dry seasons takes some getting used to if you've moved here from a part of the country with "normal" weather. Come to think of it, a lot of natives seem totally baffled by the weather too, judging from the way they carry on about it.

Our meteorological peculiarities are in large part the consequence of living "downstream" from the Pacific Ocean, that vast breeding ground of storms and currents and pressure systems.

Atmospheric pressure—the force exerted on the surface of the earth by the weight of the atmosphere—is a little tricky to conceptualize since, unlike clouds and rain and wind, it's invisible and silent; but it's worth grappling with a bit because it plays a major part in making weather. When air is heated or compressed, its molecules move more quickly and exert more pressure: the air pressure is said to be rising. Conversely, when air is cooled or allowed to expand into a larger area, its pressure decreases: falling pressure. Pressure systems are large masses of air in which the pressure is different from that of the surrounding atmosphere. A low pressure system, also called a cyclone, has winds blowing inward toward a center of minimum pressure: in the Northern Hemisphere the rotation of the winds in a low is counterclockwise, while they blow in the opposite direction in the Southern Hemisphere. In a high pressure system, or anticyclone, winds blow outward from a center of maximum pressure in a clockwise motion (again, in the Northern Hemisphere). High pressure is usually, but not always, associated with fair weather, whereas lows usually bring clouds, wind, and precipitation. Winds always blow from areas of high pressure to areas of low pressure, and the greater the difference between two adjacent pressure systems, the stronger the winds blow.

In the winter months, a persistent low pressure system off the Aleutian Islands keeps the North Pacific churning ceaselessly, and here in the Pacific Northwest we get the spillover from this turbulence. In late autumn, the swift upper-atmosphere current of wind known as the jet stream intensifies and moves south, aiming storm after storm right smack at us. Our winter storms vary in character depending on their point of origin and the direction of the steering winds. The notorious "pineapple express" flows up from the south-southwest, raising temperatures and dumping down rain for several days running. Intermittent rain showers and cooler temperatures are associated with a southwest-to-westerly storm track. This is our most prevalent winter pattern: mist, drizzle, rain, sun break, more drizzle, more rain, another break. Every now and then a storm track sweeps down from the north and elbows out over the ocean, mixing cold air from interior British Columbia with Pacific moisture. The result is snow— sometimes heavy snow—from Bellingham down to Seattle and even as far south as Portland. Luckily (or unluckily, depending on your point of view), the atmosphere rarely twists itself into this snow-bearing configuration—and even when it does, it usually snaps out of it promptly. From year to year the crown for rainiest month passes back and forth among November, December, and

January. Statistically, the day most likely to receive rain is November 19.

As days lengthen and temperatures climb, the jet stream falls apart and big storms subside. In a typical Northwest summer, a semipermanent ridge of high pressure moves north from California and parks itself off the coast of Washington, giving us a run of Mediterranean weather with prevailing northwesterly winds. Paradoxically, the ocean that fuels our winter storms keeps us dry in the summer: rain comes from warm, ascending air, but the chilly Pacific gives us just the opposite during the summer months—a shallow layer of cool, stable air that hovers between the ocean surface and a very warm layer of air above it. Since the dense, cool marine air can't rise, it doesn't bring rain. Coastal fog and overcast, yes, but no significant rainfall. July is statistically our warmest and driest month, with daytime highs averaging about 75° in Seattle and 80° in Portland, and average rainfall totaling less than an inch in western Washington and Oregon. The east side is even hotter and drier in July: average maximum temperatures approach 87° in Yakima, for example, with only .16 inch of rain. The last ten days of July and the first ten days of August are our best bet for rain-free weather.

The Pacific has a hand in determining not only seasonal rainfall patterns but also the region's characteristic temperatures. Water, which gains and loses heat more slowly than land, moderates the temperatures of adjacent terrain, keeping coastal areas mild in the winter and cool in the summer. The maritime West Coast benefits from this far more than do states along the eastern seaboard, since weather generally moves from west to east over North America. Cold and warm fronts, when they reach us, have been tempered by their passage over the ocean; the weather of coastal Maine or New Jersey, on the other hand, has traversed an entire continent, picking up the temperatures of the land below. This explains why Portland, Maine, is so much colder in the winter and often hotter in the summer than Portland, Oregon, even though they're situated at about the same latitude. The vast Pacific air conditioner not only keeps us cool in summer but also maintains humidity at a comfortable level. Even in the summer months, the Pacific waters off the West Coast remain chilly—too chilly for air passing over to pick up much moisture. The Atlantic, by contrast, warms up considerably in July and August, hence the notorious muggy, weepy summers of the mid-Atlantic states. Of course, with weather everything is relative. Seattle's August humidity is delightful if you're used to Philadelphia, but to folks from Yakima, where afternoon humidity can dip into the single digits, summertime Seattle feels damp and heavy.

With ocean to the west and a nearly unbroken wall of mountains to the east, the maritime Northwest is a basin of tepid, fairly equable weather. But the basin does occasionally crack or leak. When high pressure builds east of the Cascades in the summer months, an east wind sets up, carrying hot, dry air into the Willamette Valley and the Puget Sound lowlands. Heat waves in western Washington and Oregon rarely last more than a few days—but make no mistake, they are genuine heat waves with temperatures in the 90s or even over 100°. Part of the reason air flowing westward over the Cascade crest gets so hot is a phenomenon known as adiabatic warming: as air descends, it is compressed due to an increase of air pressure, and as it compresses it warms. The rate of warming is 5.5 degrees for every 1,000 feet of descent. This same phenomenon explains why cold snaps are seldom very cold in western Oregon and Washington: when frigid continental air gets drawn westward in the winter, it must descend the rugged slopes of the Rockies and the Cascades before it gets here. Air that is 20 below zero in Billings, Montana, is often 20 or 30 above by the time it reaches Portland. The coldest temperatures kick in when polar air skips the mountain roller-coaster ride and manages to sneak through gaps in the mountain wall—the Columbia Gorge and the Fraser River valley being the two most notable openings into our region.

And then there are the freak occurrences, occasions when Mother Nature throws in a meteorological wild card. We've had years when June was wetter than February; arctic outbreaks and heavy snows have been known to descend on us before the leaves were off the trees; Portland sometimes clocks more 90° days in July than New York City; winter storms dumping two feet of snow have paralyzed downtown Seattle more than once. These are the "weather events" that make it into the record books, newspapers, diaries, and folklore of the early settlers.

The spectacular, however, is the exception out here. Most of the time our climate is sober, mild-mannered, regular, undemonstrative. In the Midwest you read about cold fronts whipping through so suddenly and violently that chickens freeze in their tracks and riders have to be pried from their saddles, but out here the typical cold front is barely detectable—temperatures drop a few degrees, a blue hole opens up in the canopy, and then the clouds roll in again. There is not enough contrast between hot and cold air masses to ignite respectable thunderstorms, tornadoes are as scarce as blizzards, and hurricanes never happen. Two inches of snow is enough to make headlines around Puget Sound. When the mercury plummets to 25° it will top the local news broadcast in Portland. If an inch of rain falls in a day we moan about torrential monsoons, while New Orleans commonly gets an inch of rain in an hour. Our local specialty is not the gully-washer but the oxymoronic "dry rain," as an Olympia woman told newspaperman Charles Prosch at the turn of the century. It's a term I've heard myself since moving here, though I'd never encountered it before.

Northwesterners are "weather wimps," in the opinion of people from places with "real" weather. Perhaps. But I think we are also, of necessity, weather connoisseurs. Our muted seasons and cloudy skies make us sensitive to subtle changes. Day after day in winter, we read the identical forecast—rain changing to showers—yet every day is different, every period of rain has its own character. And think how many guises that meteorological standby "mostly cloudy" can assume: Now, as I write this, the late afternoon November sky is indeed mostly cloudy, but, on closer inspection, the enormous swath of mottled pearly overcast trails a lace of blue and gold at its western fringe, and there, in the time it takes to find the right words for it, the sun comes out for a final bow.

Even our fabled rain is capricious, fickle, perverse, full of dodges and whims. I've watched cloudbursts literally materialize out of the clear blue on a windy October afternoon and dissipate by sundown. Some of our so-called rainstorms dwindle to mist before they've properly gotten started, and others blur together so you don't know when one "system" has pushed through and the next one is arriving. I've seen rain in the Northwest that seems to liquefy out of the air rather than fall from the sky, rain that eats away clouds before your eyes like a celestial backspace key, rain that looks as fat as honey or as fine as rice. When you wish it would rain to green up your lawn or your garden, it holds off; when you pray for a break, it persists. Wake to a canopy of stars on a winter night; crawl back in bed convinced the next day will be sunny; rise before first light to slick pavements and weeping gray. In compensation for the recurrent moisture, we get rainbows and double rainbows and solar and lunar haloes that turn our skies into prisms. We also get to live with the thrill of meteorological uncertainty. It's a guessing game from hour to hour and microclimate to microclimate. Turn your back, drive five miles, and the weather changes. One early autumn day when we had visitors from back East, the local forecast called for sun in the morning, rain in the afternoon, then a chance of a thunderstorm followed by partial clearing. "The only thing they haven't thrown in is snow," my skeptical New York friend remarked. But we got it all, in rapid succession, and a period of hail too.

Perhaps it's because the weather out here has been the butt of so many jokes that it inspires such fascination—and clandestine pride. It's what we're known for, a regional specialty like Florida oranges or New York attitude, so we might as well revel in it. The pioneer mossbacks and webfeet have bred legions of rain poets as if in retaliation. "The rain appealed to me, and still does," writer, long-term transplant, and rain celebrant Tom Robbins told an interviewer. "It's one of the reasons why I live here. . . . It allows for prolonged periods of intimacy. It's cozy and reduces temptation. It keeps you inside where you can turn inward, rather than scattering yourself about the beach and the boulevards. And it makes the little mushrooms grow. . . ." A longtime weather columnist for the *Seattle Post-Intelligencer* spoke for many North-westerners when he admitted his preference for Seattle gloom (only "49 percent of the total possible sunshine in a year's time") over the "relentless, searing heat day after day, week after week" of such sunnier climes as Arizona and southern California. "Rain suits me," *Seattle Times* columnist Terry McDermott wrote recently. "It's the one weather event that can be almost completely appreciated indoors or out. Rain is malleable, almost infinite in its variety." The true Northwesterner doesn't own an umbrella, hardly bothers with raincoat or hat. Rain is balm, holy oil, lullaby, and gray the most mystical color in nature's palette. As Northwest transplant Brenda Peterson put it in her book *Living by Water,* "We might see how slightly we know ourselves if we don't also learn to love the shadows inside the gray and healing mists of our Northwest skies."

Humans have inhabited the Northwest for millennia, but recorded history is short. Of the long, rich period before the coming of white explorers we know almost nothing except what we can infer from native artifacts, rituals, and myths. Once the last round of glaciers retreated about 10,000 years ago, the region settled into a prolonged spell of climatic geniality—some epochs drier and warmer, some cooler and wetter, but on balance temperate, mild, and conducive to easy living for people. Natural resources were so abundant in this fertile atmosphere that the Northwest Indians never developed agriculture: though the land would have yielded handsomely, there was no need to cultivate it. Theirs was a culture of summertime gathering and wintertime contemplation. It is said that native peoples used to mark the onset of the winter rainy season by blowing whistles to signal the approach of supernatural beings. While spirits and mists drifted through the wet black boughs, the native people turned inward, devoting the rainy months to wood carving, painting, story-telling, and vision quests. One native myth explains that the weather here was once far worse: there was a time when the petulant South Wind blew constantly, bringing relentless rain, until the woodland creatures could stand it no longer; and so they ganged up and bit and clubbed the South Wind in his home until, at the verge of death, he agreed to alternate fine weather with nasty—four sunny days would follow four wet ones. A similar myth tells of a time long ago when winters were so severe that the people had to tunnel like moles to get around. In the version passed down in the Chehalis tribe, conditions got so bad one winter that a war party was dispatched to the north to kill the five snow brothers. The warriors succeeded in killing four of the five brothers, and ever since then snowy winters have been rare. According to the Hoh and Quileute peoples of the Olympic Peninsula, the rainbow is a bereft young woman who climbs the sky from beyond the ocean to search for her lost human lover. Many native peoples here have variations on a Great Flood myth, perhaps a dim racial memory of the rising of the ocean at the end of the Ice Age.

The white communities have their weather myths too, but these have not yet acquired the patina of reverence and wisdom. Our myths are more like tall tales—distorted memories of the old days when it *really* rained, family chronicles of the big Columbus Day blow of 1962 or the November freeze of 1955. We are still discovering the secrets of this environment, still getting used to its vagaries and trying to fathom its subtleties. Somehow the sky looks bigger out here; the atmosphere feels newer and sweeter and fresher, even after all the stuff we've put into it.

For centuries, the Pacific Northwest was a black void on the maps of European mariners—a region of ceaseless storms where ships were blown off course or wrecked or pushed back relentlessly to the south—and something of that pitchy, tempest-tossed mystery still clings. Our reputation for foul weather, deserved or not, invests our corner of the world with a kind of negative chic. Northwesterners have been engaged for over a century now in defending and demystifying their climate, patiently comparing rainfall totals with Philadelphia or winter temperatures with Chicago. Not all of our climatic dispatches have been disinterested or scrupulously accurate. Explorers tended to make sweeping (and often extreme) generalizations based on fleeting encounters. Various groups—politicians, regional visionaries, businessmen, local boosters—have skewed climate reports in one way or another for their own reasons. Even scientific attempts to "set the record straight" occasionally shade into defensiveness, boasting, and propaganda. So thickly encrusted is the region's meteorological reputation that out here it's impossible to discourse on what Wallace Stevens calls the "mere weather" without assuming some rhetorical stance. It's a climate that provokes strong reactions.

Certainly it has in me. My newcomer's desire to "figure out" our climate propelled me to compare myth with reality, to see what other people have made of the atmosphere over the years. My research has brought me excellent and incredibly varied company—poets and prophets, missionaries and wheat farmers, discouraged pioneers and gung-ho atmospheric scientists. As I've delved deeper into accounts written or spoken by these people, I've learned to rein in my initial zeal to "set the record straight": the record *has* been set straight time and again, and it always comes out crooked in the end. Each new attempt at disabuse drowns in skepticism, backfires, gets bogged down in the mud of disbelief. Which is why I have titled my book *Rains All the Time,* even though it obviously doesn't. That burrlike tag has been my jumping-off point. It has been wonderful to see the permutations, variations, explanations, and revisions of this notion of ceaseless rain evolve over the years.

I'll admit that I'm something of a weather nut, and the best part of researching and writing this book has been the professional excuse it gave me for indulging my obsession with the atmosphere. Our changing skies, the narratives I've read about them, and my conversations with the devoted professionals who study them have been a never-ending source of delight and inspiration for me. And I hope the same will be true for you as you turn these pages.

Chapter Two

"Stinking fogges"
"Delightful serenity"
"Tremendious wind"

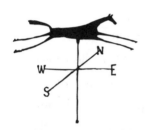

WEATHER IN THE AGE
OF EXPLORATION

I
T BEGINS, OF COURSE, WITH RAIN.
The first word to reach Europe about
the region we call the Pacific Northwest
came from one Bartolome Ferrelo, a Spanish mariner long since
faded from history. The year was 1543, the month was February,
and Ferrelo was sailing up the coast. He got as far as southern
Oregon before the rain—the incessant rain—forced him back to
the south. And so hatched the first dim image, the legend of a land
where it rains all the time. As one historian wrote, after Ferrelo
left wet "there were no further Spanish voyages recorded for sixty
years, and then none for a century and a half." Our misty coast
was sealed away from the curious, the greedy, and the adventur-
ous by incessant downpours of rain.

While the Spanish were keeping warm and dry in California,
the English slipped in. Some three and a half decades after Ferrelo

gave up on the Northwest, the first English ship penetrated our waters and our weather. April may be the cruelest month in T. S. Eliot's "The Waste Land," but here in the Pacific Northwest June is often crueler, bringing gales and showers just when we feel entitled to hope for sun and calm. Yet nothing in memory or on record approaches the cruelty of the weather that Francis Drake encountered when he sailed this way in June 1579 on his celebrated circumnavigation of the globe. Whether it arose from a strange conspiracy of the elements, a stroke of phenomenally bad luck, or a wild stretch of homesick imagination, the first published English impression of weather in the Northwest is absolutely harrowing, establishing a dank and dreary literary tradition that has endured for four centuries.

Though he is usually lumped in with the other great navigators of the Age of Exploration, Francis Drake was actually more of a political privateer—a kind of marine guerrilla fighter—than an explorer. Having honed his skills at aquatic pillaging on slave-trading voyages in the Gulf of Mexico and in skirmishes with rich Spanish ships in the Caribbean, Drake caught the eye of his ambitious and ferociously anti-Spanish monarch, Elizabeth I. In 1577, Elizabeth enlisted Drake to run a covert campaign against the Spanish colonies on America's Pacific coast, outfitting him with five ships and 166 men. Once he reached the Northwest coast, Drake was also supposed to search for the Northwest Passage, the fabled transcontinental waterway that European and American explorers pursued as an ever elusive grail from the time of Columbus until the dawn of the nineteenth century. Drake embarked from Plymouth, England, late in the autumn of 1577 and almost immediately ran afoul of bad luck and bad weather. It took him a year to get to the west coast of Central America, in the course of which he suppressed a mutiny, and when he limped into the tiny port of Guatulco (not far from Acapulco) in the spring of 1579, he had but a single ship left of his original fleet— his flagship, the *Golden Hind*. Undeterred by his losses, Drake proceeded up the Pacific coast, plundering all Spanish possessions and ships that fell in his path, including the plum galleon *Nuestra Señora de la Concepción,* which yielded up a mighty cache of silver and gold—a hoard estimated at over ₤126,000, approximately half of the yearly revenue of the English Crown at the time. Progress northward was rapid, and by early June the *Golden Hind* had reached what is now the California-Oregon border. It was here that the weather turned suddenly and viciously inclement. Francis Fletcher, the ship's chaplain and the author of *The World Encompassed by Sir Francis Drake,* published in 1628 and still considered the most complete and reliable record of the voyage, gave this account of the freakish weather: "[On June 3, 1579] we came into 42. deg. of North latitude, where in the night following, we found such alteration of heate, into extreame and nipping cold, that our men in generall did grievously complaine thereof, some of them feeling their healths much impaired thereby." To "the great admiration" of the entire ship's company, the next day was no warmer than the miserable night had been: "The pinching and biting aire, was nothing altered; the very roapes of our ship were stiffe, and the raine which fell, was an unnatural congealed and frozen substance, so that we seemed rather to be in the frozen Zone, then any way so neere unto the sun, or these hotter climates."

Drake buoyed the crew's spirits as best he could with "comfortable speeches" and "other good and profitable perswasions," but to no avail. The farther north they sailed, "the more extremitie of cold did sease upon us," and a stiff north wind "directly bent against us," making progress all but impossible. Even at anchor there was no respite from the "many extreme gusts and flawes that beate upon us." The rare calms brought little relief, for the instant the wind ceased "there followed the most vile, thicke, and stinking fogges, against which the sea prevailed nothing, till the gusts of wind againe removed them, which brought with them such extremeity and violence when they came, that there was no dealing or resisting against them." Fletcher reported with English phlegm that in the face of such weather "a sudden and great discouragement seased upon the mindes of our men, and they were possessed with a great mislike" for the land that Drake had christened New Albion. Nonetheless, the *Golden Hind* inched northward, possibly getting as far north as 48 degrees of latitude—near today's Washington-Canada border—before Drake finally gave up any hope of discovering the Northwest Passage and returned to the vicinity of present-day San Francisco. (Historians are still debating Drake's West Coast itinerary, especially the question of how far north he went and where in California he anchored.)

Fogs, even "vile, thicke, and stinking fogges," are not uncommon off the northern California and southern Oregon coast in early June, but how to account for the "extreame and nipping cold" that congealed water onto the ship's ropes and froze the crew's meat before they could eat it? Fletcher, "inquir[ing] into the causes" of the cold with the new scientific reasoning of his day, noted that the weather change came on quite suddenly as the *Golden Hind* sailed north, with but two degrees of latitude separating the warm southern zone from the frigid zone to the north. This led him to consider the possibility that the English crew may have been more "sensible of the cold" because their prolonged sojourn in the tropics had opened their pores and softened their bodies. But he promptly dismissed this idea on the grounds that "the naturall inhabitants of the place" were suffering from the cold just as much as were the English mariners: the Indians came "shivering to us in their warme furres, crowding close together, body to body, to receive heate one of another." The true explanation, he asserted, lay in geography and weather patterns. Remarking that "high and snow-covered mountaines" dominate the region where the Asian and American continents come together in the distant north, Fletcher reasoned that the prevailing north and northwest winds "send abroad their frozen nimphes, to the infecting of the whole aire with this insufferable sharpnesse: not permitting the Sunne, no, not in the pride of his heate, to dissolve that congealed matter and snow." He concluded, rationally enough, that the northerly winds of the Northwest summer were to blame for the region's awful climate: "Hence comes the generall squalidnesse and barrennesse of the countrie; hence comes it, that in the middest of their summer, the snow hardly departeth even from their very doores, but is never taken away from their hils at all; hence come those thicke mists and most stinking fogges." Fletcher, of course, got it very wrong—winds from the north and northwest normally bring us fair weather during the summer months—but apparently the weather was anything but normal in the summer of 1579.

Could Fletcher have been stretching the truth a bit—or just plain fabricating—perhaps in order to deflect attention from the fact that Drake failed to find the Northwest Passage, indeed failed to get very far north? Was this chapter of *The World Encompassed* an Elizabethan snow job? Historians are still not certain. In a fascinating pamphlet entitled "Question: Did Sir Francis Drake Land on any Part of the Oregon Coast," published in Portland, Oregon, in 1907, one R. M. Brereton compiled and assessed the evidence and opinions pro and con. Strongly on the con side was Robert Greenhow's 1845 volume *The History of Oregon and California*. Greenhow scoffed at Fletcher's claim that the *Golden Hind* sailed north through six degrees of latitude in two days—a difficult feat, Greenhow pointed out, in the face of constant north winds and storms. And he dismissed the reports of the "extreame and nipping cold" as "direct falsehoods." This was too much for Brereton, who promptly rose to Fletcher's defense. He pointed out that a Spanish sailor named Juan Rodriguez Cabrillo, sailing out of Port de Navidad (now Port-au-Prince, Haiti), also encountered extreme cold when he reached the California-Oregon coast in March 1544. "It may be that a much colder cycle prevailed in those latitudes in the sixteenth century than what has been known by white men since," Brereton concluded reasonably. "It may be that the Japan gulf stream had a more western direction in the sixteenth century, which would have made the coast climate of Oregon and northern California colder. Earthquakes and alterations therefrom in the level of the ocean bed would probably cause diversion in the general course of this stream." It's an intriguing hypothesis.

Brereton's earthquakes are speculative, but there was indeed "a much colder cycle" in the sixteenth century. The Little Ice Age, as the period between 1430 and 1850 is called, lowered temperatures significantly in the Northern Hemisphere. During the coldest spells, temperatures were as much as 5.4 degrees colder than our current averages. England's Thames River began freezing over during the winters of the 1560s and continued to grow solid regularly throughout the seventeenth century. During the memorably severe winter of 1607–8, the ice was so thick and hard that Londoners held a Frost Fair on the frozen river, a tradition that continued into the 1680s. Drake's voyage to our stormy waters fell right in the middle of the Little Ice Age. So it's possible that the congealed and frozen "raine" and "stinking fogges" of which Fletcher wrote were typical of June weather in the Pacific Northwest at the time. As weather historian Steve Mierzejewski noted in *Footprints on the Rivers,* his fascinating study of past Northwest winters, snow has been reported in western Oregon in May as recently as 1966, so June snow is certainly within the range of possibilities, especially during the notoriously chilly year of 1579. Drake, Mierzejewski argued, likely encountered what we now call mixed precipitation—slushy snow, hail, and rain—but that the weather *seemed* colder than it actually was because everyone on board was so thoroughly miserable. Certainly the misery in Fletcher's account has the sterling ring of truth.

Fletcher's history of Drake's voyage stood as the primary document of Northwest weather for two centuries. The image of the Pacific Northwest as an uninhabitable blot—remote, freezing, wet, stormy, ugly, barren—lodged itself in the English imagination. "In this place was no abiding for us," stated Fletcher as the *Golden Hind* retreated southward, and his countrymen saw no reason to question this conclusion. For the seventeenth and most of the eighteenth century the region was viewed primarily as an enigmatic obstacle—a mountainous mass of green and white that stubbornly obscured the coveted Northwest Passage. The few exploring parties that did come this way sailed out of Mexico under Spanish colors. But since the Spanish preferred to keep the records of their explorations to themselves, "their discoveries, as far as the rest of Europe was concerned, were scarcely discoveries at all," as historian Carlos A. Schwantes put it.

It wasn't until England's heroic circumnavigator James Cook made his third voyage around the globe, starting in 1776, that another good account of climatic conditions in the Pacific Northwest was produced. Cook was cut from an altogether different cloth than Drake. A man of humble origin and modest demeanor who rose through the ranks of the English navy, Cook was a kind of Renaissance man of the sea—a naval officer, the discoverer of vast tracts of the globe including sections of Australia and New Zealand, New Caledonia, Hawaii, and the coast of Alaska, a scrupulous cartographer, and a self-educated scientist who could hold his own in mathematics, astronomy, and medicine. Revered by his crews for his kindness and wisdom, Cook pioneered the use of citrus fruit and sauerkraut in combating scurvy, and he defied the custom of what one historian calls his "savage age" by insisting on relatively light punishments and clean, dry clothes for his men. When he embarked on his third and final voyage, Cook had already been around the world twice, having sailed both east and west out of England. This time he bore with him sealed

instructions from the British Admiralty to locate the long-sought
Northwest Passage, for which discovery Parliament was then
offering £20,000 in reward money (well over half a million dollars by today's standards). Such was the explorer's prestige in the
late eighteenth century and such the importance accorded his
mission that the Americans, though fighting a war to throw off
English rule, agreed to give Cook's ships free passage and to treat
the explorer and his crew "with all civility and kindness, affording
them as common friends to mankind."

Cook embarked from Plymouth, England, ten days after the
signing of the Declaration of Independence, following the prevailing winds southwestward to the eastern tip of Brazil. After
recrossing the South Atlantic and rounding the Cape, Cook
dipped farther south to explore the Antarctic Islands and then
continued on to New Zealand. In January 1778, he came upon his
most delightful discovery, the Hawaiian archipelago, which he
named the Sandwich Islands in honor of John Montagu, Earl of
Sandwich. There was no lingering in the "very comfortable" climate of Kauai and Oahu, however, for the Northwest Passage still
beckoned; on February 3, 1778, Cook's ships, the *Resolution* and
the *Discovery,* set sail for North America. By March 1, Cook had
reached the 49th parallel of latitude, which, as he knew, was
about as far north as Drake had gotten. In his journal he wrote of
his surprise at how different the weather was from what Drake
had encountered: "It was remarkable that we should still be
attended with such moderate and mild weather so far to the
northward at this time of year. We can assign no reason why Sir
Francis Drake should have met with such severe cold about this
latitude in the month of June. Viscaino [a Spanish explorer who

had sailed these waters in 1602 and 1603], who was near the same place in the depth of winter, says little of the cold. . . ."

Cook soon found that his assessment of Pacific Northwest weather as "moderate and mild" was a bit premature, for as he approached the coast a storm came up, "blowing in squalls with hail and sleet, and the weather being thick and hazy I stood out to sea." John Ledyard, a Connecticut adventurer sailing with Cook who kept his own log of the voyage, gave this terse but vivid account of the conditions along the Northwest coast: "The weather was cold, the gales of wind were successive and strong, and sometimes very violent. Our ships complained. We were short of water, and had an unknown coast to explore." The "succession of adverse winds and boisterous weather," as Cook termed it, endured for the better part of two weeks, twice forcing the ships off course. Oregon's Cape Foulweather, a jump north of what was to become Newport, got its name at the start of this blow, and the "thick and hazy" conditions may well explain why Cook sailed right by the mouth of the Columbia River. Bad weather was not, however, responsible for an even bigger geographical blunder on Cook's part: his failure to detect the opening to the Strait of Juan de Fuca. His journal reported that the weather finally turned fair on March 21, allowing the ships to sail in fairly close to the shore, where they spotted "a small opening which flattered us with the hopes of finding a harbor. These hopes lessened as we drew nearer, for the opening was closed by low land. On this account I called the point of land to the north of it Cape Flattery. It lies in the latitude 48°15' north. It is in this very latitude where we now were that geographers have placed the pretended strait of Juan de Fuca. We saw nothing like it, nor is there the least probability that ever any such thing existed." Had he not been killed the following year by angry natives on Hawaii, Cook would have lived to sorely regret that last sentence, for "the pretended strait" was soon to be thoroughly explored and charted by one of his own company, a midshipman named George Vancouver. How so gifted an explorer as Cook could have missed so large a geographic feature as the twenty-mile-wide entrance to the Strait of Juan de Fuca, especially since the express purpose of his mission was to locate an opening in this very vicinity, remains one of the mysteries of the Age of Exploration. It was a serious error—one that "cost Britain sole possession of the Pacific Northwest," as writer Robert Cantwell put it.

Cook cruised on northward, harboring a few days later in Nootka Sound off what would shortly be named Vancouver Island, and devoted the month of April to repairing his ships. It was enough time to give him a fair sampling of our early spring weather: "When ever it rained with us Snow fell on the Neighbouring hills, the Clemate is however infinately milder than on the East coast of America under the same parallel of latitude. The Mercury in the Thermometre never even in the night fell lower than 42 and very often in the day it rose to 60; no such thing as frost was perceived in any of the low ground, on the Contrary Vegetation had made considerable progress, I met with grass that was already above a foot long. . . ." This has a familiar ring to it—certainly more reminiscent of today's weather than Drake's June sleet storm. Cook spent the summer exploring the northern reaches of the West Coast, eventually sailing through the Bering Strait and confirming that this channel did indeed separate Asia from America. In the fall he returned to the Sandwich Islands, and it was there that he was killed by aggrieved natives in revenge for his rough treatment of their chief.

The real significance of Cook's brush with the Northwest lay neither in geography nor in climate, but in furs. Ledyard was positively rhapsodic on the subject: "The light in which this country will appear most to advantage respects the variety of its animals, and the richness of their furr. They have foxes, sables, hares, marmosets, ermines, weazles, bears, wolves, deer, moose, dogs, otters, beavers, and a species of weazle called the glutton." Ledyard sorely regretted that they did not carry off more pelts, for, as he wrote, beaver skins "which did not cost the purchaser sixpence sterling sold in China for 100 dollars." Equally prized were the fine soft sea otter skins of the Northwest, especially the older pelts, which the Chinese considered the most desirable. Ledyard confessed frankly that Cook's crew would "most certainly" have snapped up more pelts "had we known of meeting the opportunity of disposing of them to such an astonishing profit." News of "astonishing profit" always travels fast, and Western adventurers were soon swarming into the region to trap and trade. Thus commenced the region's first major commercial enterprise.

Fur traders had little time to spare for chronicling the weather: they kept their eyes fixed on the goal of amassing the greatest number of pelts at the lowest price, getting them to market as swiftly as possible, and moving on quickly when the supply dwindled. But the late eighteenth century does yield one more splendid weather document—the journals kept by George Vancouver during his two-month sojourn in and around Puget Sound in 1792. Once again, finding the Northwest Passage was the primary reason for the voyage: Vancouver was instructed "to examine the northwest coast of America from 30° to 60° in order to *facilitate intercourse by water communication* with the opposite side of the continent." That proved an impossible mission, but Vancouver did succeed where Cook, his former commanding officer, had failed: he penetrated the elusive Strait of Juan de Fuca, falling upon the adjacent network of waterways as upon a chest of treasure. Every reach and cove, each twist in the shoreline disclosed new beauties and raised fresh hopes. Vancouver tirelessly pursued channel after channel, bay after bay—an onerous task indeed given the tortuous, island-studded geography of the region. Though he was ultimately frustrated in his quest for the passage, Vancouver was enchanted with the Puget Sound country, especially with its weather—the first fair weather any European had reported finding in the Northwest. The bachelor captain sounded rather like a character out of Jane Austen (who was sixteen at the time) as he catalogued the virtues of the bucolic scene: "The country before us presented a most luxuriant landscape," he wrote while proceeding north past the mouth of the still-undiscovered Columbia, "and was probably not a little heightened in beauty by the weather that prevailed . . . pleasant weather, so favourable to our examination of the coast." After a bout of "thick rainy weather" toward the end of April, fair skies returned in May, and Vancouver's party entered the straits under ideal conditions: "The delightful serenity of the weather permitted our seeing this inlet to great advantage." (The same spell of fair spring weather prevailed when one Robert Gray, a Boston ship captain and the first American citizen to circumnavigate the globe, finally succeeded in sailing into the mouth of the Columbia just a few days later: "Fresh breezes and pleasant weather," reads the ship's log for

May 10. Gray sailed fifteen miles upstream, gathered a fortune in sea otter pelts, and named the river for his ship, the *Columbia Rediva*.)

"Delightful" was the word that came most readily to Vancouver's pen in connection with our weather: utterly absent in his report is the damp, dark, stormy frustration of earlier accounts. Here was a man of the world who surveyed the passing scene with a connoisseur's appreciation and an English commander's sense of entitlement. Thus on Protection Island (just west of Port Townsend, at the entrance to Discovery Bay), he remarked: "Our attention was immediately called to a land-scape, almost as enchantingly beautiful as the most elegantly finished pleasure grounds in Europe. . . ." And he waxed even more rhapsodic while sailing out of New Dungeness on the splendid morning of May 2: "The delightful serenity of the weather greatly aided the beautiful scenery that was now presented; the surface of the sea was perfectly smooth, and the country before us exhibited every thing that bounteous nature could be expected to draw into one point of view. As we had no reason to imagine that this country had ever been indebted for any of its decorations to the hand of man, I could not possibly believe that any uncultivated country had ever been discovered exhibiting so rich a picture." "Torrents of rain" on May 9 dampened his enthusiasm a touch, and also account for the naming of Foulweather Bluff (a thumb of land west of Skunk Bay that guards the entrance to Hood Canal). But Vancouver promptly recovered his good spirits and graciously rose to defend "the general serenity of the weather," which showered no more rain than was "absolutely requisite in the spring of the year to bring forward the annual productions."

Archibald Menzies, the expedition's botanist, was equally smitten: "A Traveller wandering over these unfrequented Plains is regaled with a salubrious & vivifying air impregnated with the balsamic fragrance of the surrounding Pinery, while his mind is eagerly occupied every moment on new objects & his senses rivetted on the enchanting variety of the surrounding scenery where the softer beauties of Landscape are harmoniously blended in majestic grandeur with the wild & romantic to form an interesting & picturesque prospect on every side." Menzies may have tripped over his adjectives, but he was an astute botanist, remembered today for identifying the madrona tree, that beloved native of the Northwest coast, which bears his name—*Arbutus menziesii*.

Vancouver summed up his admiration for the region's climate, topography, and future promise with an elegant flourish of late Augustan prose: "To describe the beauties of this region will on some future occasion, be a very grateful task to the pen of a skilful panegyrist. The serenity of the climate, the innumerable pleasing landscapes, and the abundant fertility that unassisted nature puts forth, require only to be enriched by the industry of man with villages, mansions, cottages, and other buildings, to render it the most lovely country that can be imagined; whilst the labour of the inhabitants would be amply rewarded, in the bounties which nature seems ready to bestow on cultivation." He made the Northwest sound like an embryonic England just waiting for the civilizing exertions of the squire, the parson, and the yeoman.

While Vancouver lavished praise on the country surrounding the Strait of Juan de Fuca and Admiralty Inlet, he was slightly less enthralled by the "landscapes" of the inland sea that he named to reward the diligence of his twenty-eight-year-old lieutenant,

Peter Puget. Evidently Vancouver was growing weary of the monotonous, impenetrable, seemingly endless shoreline "presenting one uninterrupted wilderness" (always a word with negative connotations for the English). When a June squall blew up over Vashon Island, Vancouver succumbed to a fit of despondency: "Our residence here was truly forlorn; an awful silence pervaded the gloomy forests, whilst animated nature seemed to have deserted the neighboring country. . . ."

Vancouver gives us the first detailed picture in English of a Northwest spring and summer—a glowing watercolor in greens and pale blues. Winter is absent from his canvas. But we do get a fleeting glimpse of the inclement season in the journals kept by one of Vancouver's men, a crew member of the *Chatham,* the armed tender that accompanied Vancouver's sloop *Discovery*. This seaman, whose name has not come down to us, had heard through the nautical grapevine that a "bad season" sets in on the Northwest coast during the autumn, during which the wind blows incessantly from the southeast bringing "gales, with constant rain and Fogs . . . [and] three months of incessant hard rain. Very little snow falls on the low ground nor is the Frost at all intense, the Ice on no part of their Lakes or Rivers being above an inch thick." Vancouver's party got a little taste of the "bad season" at Nootka Sound in late September and early October, and that taste was enough. On October 12 Vancouver weighed anchor and headed south to California.

A great, great deal more about the "bad season" in the Pacific Northwest was to emerge in print soon after Captains Meriwether Lewis and William Clark led their famous Corps of Discovery over the Rockies, down the Columbia, and out to the margin of the Pacific Ocean in November 1805. The particulars of the Lewis and Clark expedition are well known: The conception of the mission by President Thomas Jefferson after he pulled off the real estate deal of the millennium by acquiring the 800,000-square-mile Louisiana Territory for a mere $15 million; the engagement of the two eminently suitable and wonderfully companionable military men to lead the Corps of Discovery— Lewis, Jefferson's thirty-year-old private secretary, and Clark, Lewis's friend and former commanding officer, a man four years his senior who had less education but more experience in combat, woods lore, and roughing it; the departure of the exploring party from the camp near St. Louis on May 14, 1804; the incredible good fortune that took the group of thirty to forty unmarried soldiers, a mixed-blood hunter, and a slave through wild, largely uncharted, spectacularly varied terrain with the loss of but a single man. Lewis and Clark's success, good sense, and good nature (which they extended to the native peoples they encountered) have made them the most admired of America's explorers, especially in the states through which they trekked.

Still, despite the familiarity of the Lewis and Clark expedition, a few particulars bear looking into. Although Lewis and Clark, unlike the British and Spanish explorers who preceded them to the Northwest, came overland and approached from the east, they shared with their predecessors the same fundamental goal: the discovery of the Northwest Passage. Jefferson's instructions were explicit in this regard: the "Corps of Discovery of the Northwest" was "to explore the Missouri river, & such principal stream of it, as, by it's course and communication with the waters of the Pacific ocean, whether the Columbia, Oregan, Colorado or any other river may offer the most direct & practicable water communication across this continent for the purposes of commerce." *For the purposes of commerce:* the same motive that drew Cook up to the Bering Strait and sent Vancouver poking down every twist and turn of Puget Sound. Facilitating trade, however, was not the sole inducement, for Jefferson was also eager to have the captains fill in the vast blank spaces of the West—its topography, its flora and fauna, its native populations, and its weather. The instructions regarding weather were explicit and detailed: they were to observe and document "climate, as characterized by the thermometer, by the proportions of rainy, cloudy, and clear days, by lightning, hail, snow, ice, by the access and recess of frost, by the winds prevailing at different seasons, the dates at which particular plants put forth or lose their flowers or leaf, times of appearance of particular birds, reptiles or insects," and so on. Jefferson was himself a serious and lifelong weather enthusiast, and these are precisely the climatic data that he religiously monitored each day and recorded in his journals and garden books.

Duly equipped with weather instruments (all of which, unfortunately, got lost or broken in the course of the journey), Lewis and Clark carried out their meteorological orders in every particular, and their eight-volume journal fairly teems with weather data: the frigid temperatures they encountered during their winter at Mandan, North Dakota; the "astonishing violence" of the wind on the Great Plains; the "remarkably dry and pure" air of the arid West; the eternal snow that gleamed on the jagged peaks of the Rockies. Once the Corps of Discovery reached the

Pacific Northwest, the meteorological aspect of the narrative took on an almost epic quality as the rainy season closed in on them with all its majestic, roiling, windblown, elemental, bone-drenching wetness.

The awful truth about our winters dawned on the captains slowly. September 1805 found them in the Bitterroot Mountains of Idaho, with clouds and rain the first week and snow by mid-month. Clark, September 16: "Began to Snow about 3 hours before Day and continued all day   the Snow in the morning 4 inches deep on the old Snow, and by night we found it from 6 to 8 inches deep. . . . I have been wet and as cold in every part as I ever was in my life, indeed I was at one time fearfull my feet would freeze in the thin Mockirsons which I wore. . . ." This was but a foretaste of the discomforts to come. By October they had reached the Columbia River, and in the course of the month they drifted and paddled westward through the stark, treeless, desert clarity of the Columbian plains into the gaping jaws of the Pacific Northwest rainy season. On October 30 they were at the future site of the Bonneville Dam: "The day proved cloudy dark and disagreeable with some rain all day which kept us wet. . . ." The next day: "Cloudy rainey disagreeable morning." On November 3, the thick fog cleared for a few hours, revealing a glimpse of Mount Hood. Encamped near the mouth of the river on November 5: "Rained all the after part of last night, rain continued this morning, I [s]lept but verry little last night for the noise Kept [up] dureing the whole of the night by the Swans, Geese, white & Grey Brant Ducks &c. on a Small Sand Island close under the Lard. Side; they were emensely noumerous, and their noise horid. . . . The day proved cloudy with rain the greater part of it, we are all wet cold and disagreeable . . ." The word "disagreeable" now begins to crop up with increasing frequency, far surpassing Vancouver's vernal refrain of "delightful." Disagreeable: a polite euphemism covering a bottomless well of sodden disgust. Moderate rain continued all day on November 7, but the misery of the weather was relieved temporarily by the sighting of the ocean— at last, a glimpse of the destination they had been struggling to reach for a year and a half. "Great joy in camp," reads Clark's famous journal entry, "we are in *view* of the *Ocian,* this great Pacific Octean which we been so long anxious to See. and the roreing or noise made by the waves brakeing on the rockey Shores (as I suppose) may be heard disti[n]ctly." Emotion had obviously undermined Clark's already tottering spelling and grammar. (Scholars have pointed out that the explorers were actually viewing Gray's Bay, a few miles from the mouth of the Columbia, and not the Pacific Ocean proper—but they were indeed very close.)

Next day the joy subsided and it was back to the same old disagreeable rain, the misery of the weather now aggravated by a steep, precarious encampment that afforded no protection from the rising waters of the river and no level ground on which to store the baggage. "The rainey weather continued without a longer intermition than 2 hours at a time," Clark recorded with dripping amazement on November 15; "from the 5th [of November] in the morng. untill the 16th is *eleven* days rain, and the most disagreeable time I have experenced confined on a tempiest coast wet, where I can neither git out to hunt, return to a better situation, or proceed on." And so it went for nearly five miserably soggy months: more rain and stiff winds as the explorers finally succeeded in moving the camp down to the mouth of the river near the Pacific shore; rain, "tremendious wind," and a ceaseless, tormenting roar of ocean waves as they clung for several days to the spit of land on the exposed southwest Washington shore ("the sea . . . roars like a repeeted roling thunder," wrote Clark, "and have rored in that way ever since . . . we arrived in sight of the Great Western Ocian, I cant say Pasific as since I have seen it, it has been the reverse"); rain and wind finally driving them across the river and down into Oregon, where they found a new campsite in a more sheltered spot a short distance inland; rain or showers plaguing them every day during the construction of Fort Clatsop; rain and pervasive dampness rotting their clothes, moccasins, blankets, robes, and animal hides, and breeding legions of fleas. "O! how horriable is the day," Clark wailed at one point as yet another storm blew in and drenched the camp with rain and churned-up river water. Eventually Clark ceased to detail the duration or severity of the rainstorms and merely jotted phrases in his journal: "The rain &c.," "rained last night as usial." At winter's end, Clark made a weather tally and calculated that there had been only twelve days without rain and only six days with sunshine (sunshine, he added in disgust, was a relative term, for even "when the sun is said to shine or the weather fair it is to be understood that it barely casts a shadow, and that the atmosphere is haizy of a milkey white colour"). Surely this winter of 1805–6 must rank with the wettest, gloomiest, most utterly disagreeable Northwest rainy seasons of all time.

More welcome than the rains, though just as surprising to the captains, was the relative mildness of the winter temperatures. "I am confident that the climate here is much warmer than in the same parallel of Latitude on the Atlantic Ocean," wrote Lewis in his meteorological notes, "tho' how many degrees is now out of my power to determine [since the last thermometer had broken in the Idaho mountains]. Since our arrival in this neighborhood of the 7th of November, we have experienced one slight white frost only which happened on the morning of the 16th of that month. We have yet seen no ice, and the weather so warm that we are obliged to cure our meat with smoke and fire to save it." He noted with astonishment that in mid-January "various flies and insects" were "alive and in motion," although a spell of cold weather set in toward the end of January, and 6 inches of snow covered the ground by January 27; the ground remained white until February, and light snow came at intervals through mid-March. Both Lewis and Clark were also struck by the extreme and abrupt variability of Northwest winter weather: "The changes of the weather are exceedingly sudden," they noted on January 1; "sometimes tho' seldom the sun is visible for a few moments the next it hails & rains, then ceases, and remains cloudy the wind blows and it again rains . . . these visicitudes of the weather happen two three or more times a day." All in all, "a surpriseing climate," as Clark summed up before the Corps of Discovery left Fort Clatsop for good and headed gratefully back East on March 23, 1806.

The journals of Lewis and Clark, which were first published in 1814 in a highly condensed and heavily edited form in Nicholas Biddle's *History of the Exploration Under the Command of Captains Lewis and Clark,* lodged the Northwest "bad season" firmly in the public's mind. What had previously been sailors' rumors or trap-

pers' tall tales was now established as fact: five months of ceaseless rain. After Lewis and Clark, Americans knew that the way
west was long and hard and mountainous, that no smooth shining
Northwest Passage linked the Missouri with the Pacific, that the
fabled Pacific itself was storm-ridden and violent and shrouded in
damp. "The West toward which the explorers of three centuries
had groped through darkness was now brought to light," wrote
John Logan Allen in his adept study *Passage Through the Garden:
Lewis and Clark and the Image of the American Northwest*. "But it was
the light of reality and the shattering of a dream. . . . The West
was not golden, it was gray." Nonetheless, Americans wanted to
follow where Lewis and Clark had led and see it for themselves.
At first they came in a trickle and then, after the opening of the
Oregon Trail in the 1840s, in a flood. Thousands turned south
once they got out here, and settled in the hot sunny valleys of California. But many others remained in the Northwest, to try their
luck farming along the banks of the Willamette and logging in the
forests of the Cascade and Olympic mountain ranges. Settlers'
weather, as we'll see, bore a very different aspect from the
weather encountered by explorers.

Summer

I was astounded when I discovered that the house I
was about to buy in Seattle had a built-in sprinkler system.
"What on earth is *that* for?" I asked the kindly old gent
from whom we were buying the place. He fixed me with
that quizzical gaze I would soon know well— the gaze with
which a Northwest native or longtime resident plumbs the
depths of a newcomer's ignorance. "Summers are actually
quite dry here," he finally replied blandly. "Mediterranean,
in fact. Some years you'll have to water the lawn every other
day." "You don't say," I mumbled, all the while thinking, *Yeah,
right, tell me another one. He's probably just trying to make me
feel better for having forked over my life's savings and then some.*
"Mediterranean" in connection with Seattle struck me as one
more bit of real estate agent's jargon, like "territorial view"
or "original period details." True, at this critical juncture in
my life I had spent a grand total of seven days in Seattle;
and true, five of those seven days were rainless. But the idea
of running a sprinkler in the city notorious for precipitation
struck me as a tad farfetched.

You should have seen my water bill last July.

"Clouds? Never heard of them, never seen them," I wrote
on July 8 in my weather journal, as the lawn turned crisp and
brown around the edges:

> Just as the natives always insist, it rained on Indepen-
> dence Day—actually just a sprinkle this year, though
> we had some steady drizzle the day before. But by July
> 5 it was lovely and fair, and it's been that way ever

since. Saturday, July 6, dawned perfect and warm and
cloudless—we spent the day toasting and desiccating
on the beach at Dungeness Spit on the Strait of Juan
de Fuca, hardly a breeze till evening, felt like about
80°. Perfect summer day. Yesterday, more of the same,
only five or so degrees warmer—mid-80s and felt
like Arizona with searing sun by early afternoon. Hot,
dry, still. Endless summer weather—cannot imagine
another season. Soil is dry. Air is dry. And luckily that
haze we sometimes get hasn't kicked in yet, or hardly
at all, so the mountains are still fairly sharp, snow
patches still visible. The long, long lingering afterglow
of evening is wonderful—I was reading outside with
no artificial light till 9 P.M. Today, another hot dry
cloudless day. High summer. Maybe we're in for one
of those perfect summers. Rain and clouds unimagin-
able. As Kate just said, "It's hard to fathom how miserable it can be." Forecast is calling for more fair weather
ahead, first cooling a bit, then heat building in again.

After four years here, I still can't quite believe our long
unbroken spells of summer sun are *real*—and, in fact, typical.
But to my mind the finest, and most unexpected, pleasure
of a Northwest summer is the low humidity level. Newcomers like me take one look at the proximity of ocean and
the wetness of earth after winter rains and conclude that
humidity will teem like mildew come summer warmth. But
the Pacific waters near our coastlines remain too cool, even
at the height of summer, to feed much moisture into the
air masses passing over. The combination of cool ocean and
persistent high pressure results in a run of Eden-like weather:
afternoon highs in the mid-70s west of the Cascades, with

light afternoon breezes and cool nights. And this pattern, once it sets up, can persist for weeks or even months at a time.

"This Oregon is a noble country!" Yankee wayfarer Theodore Winthrop declared in a letter to his family back East on July 12, 1853, less than half a century after Lewis and Clark decamped in sodden disgust. "The summer climate is almost perfection, and the winter, though rainy, not severe or disagreeable. It offers a grand field for a man who is either a world in himself, or who can have his own world about him." And writer John Mortimer Murphy waxed even more eloquent about the "cooling breezes" and "most delicious temperature" of our "season of *dolce far niente*" in one of the first travel pieces about the Pacific Northwest ever published; it appeared in the very genteel *Appleton's Journal* of November 1877.

Phil Church, a former chairman of the University of Washington department of atmospheric sciences, gave the scientific explanation for this "most agreeable" summer weather in *Weatherwise* magazine: "In the summer the huge Pacific high pressure area is farthest north and the outflowing air, warming as it descends, reaches the Washington coast as a wind from the northwest. As this wind approaches the coast it is cooled by contact with the North Pacific water." Church remarked upon how surprised newcomers are to find that the prevailing northwest winds of summer bring in fair, warm weather— it's just the opposite on the East Coast, where northwest winds are brisk in summer and relatively uncommon. "The ever balmy north west breeze," one nineteenth-century sojourner breathed in ecstasy as he basked near the Strait of Juan de Fuca, "in summer, gently sweeping up and spreading over this vast region, giving that pulsating life and health that arms men to do big things. . . ." The *duration* of our summertime weather patterns is also remarkable: back East, you typically get a day or two of warm dry weather, after which the

temperature and humidity start to climb until they become
unbearable, and then, if you're lucky, a thunderstorm clears
the air. But here in the Northwest, as one meteorologist told
me, "you can go for forty to sixty days with no clouds or
precipitation. The upper ridge is stable; there are no weather
systems pushing through." In the long hot summer of 1958
Seattle stayed dry for forty-five days, then got .01 inch of
rain, then suffered through sixteen more days of drought. The
summer of 1967 brought seventy dry days.

Had *Appleton's Journal* writer John Mortimer Murphy
crossed the Cascades to visit Yakima or Walla Walla during
his summertime ramble through Washington, he might have
found the weather somewhat less conducive to *dolce far niente*:
daytime highs in the upper 80s, 90s, and even 100s are the
rule in this part of the Northwest. Wahluke (near Hanford)
recorded a high temperature of 118° on July 24, 1928, and
Prineville (in Crook County, Oregon) beat that by a degree
on July 29, 1898. A vivid account of what it feels like to be
outdoors in this kind of heat appears in the journal of Caroline C. Leighton, a New Englander who lived and traveled
around the West Coast in the 1860s and 1870s. Late in the
summer of 1866, Leighton and her husband were journeying
overland from Fort Colville to Seattle—through "the wildest
desert country," as she put it, with awesome scenery and
awesome heat: "The extreme heat . . . seemed to intensify
every thing in us, even our power of enjoyment, notwithstanding the discomfort of it. The thermometer marked
117° in the shade. I felt as if I had never before known what
breezes and shadows and streams were."

Extreme heat also shimmers through the novels of Allis
McKay, a writer who grew up in eastern Washington during
the first half of this century. Her first novel, *They Came to a
River* (1941), set in the apple-growing country of the Columbia

River valley, conjured up heat that was "a palpable thing, like a blanket, to push against with bare legs; it lay on everything in invisible heaps. At a distance, you could see it: it shimmered. Close up, it was just a thick nothingness that rubbed against your cheek, that squinted your eyes shut. . . . The heat was a sort of thing, cruelly friendly, living a rough life of its own. . . . At seven o'clock the sun went down, and the whole dry hot earth felt instantly as if it had been wiped with a cool sponge, dipped in green and lavender." I felt this blanket of heat myself the first time I drove down into the Columbia River valley out of the Okanogan Highlands in August. As soon as I got out of the air-conditioned car, the heat became overwhelming, smothering. The air was dry but strangely heavy; it felt as if you'd need an oar to paddle through it. And it just sat there, with never a lick of wind to stir things around. It did indeed, as Caroline Leighton wrote, seem to intensify everything.

Heat of this intensity is rare but not unknown west of the mountains. Seattle has hit 100° more than once, and in Portland, which is generally five to seven degrees warmer than Seattle in the summer and cooler by the same amount in the winter, the record high is 107°, set at the airport on August 8, 1981, and downtown on July 2, 1942. In July 1996, Portland had a record twelve days with readings in the 90s, and in 1985 Portland's July set a heat record with daily temperatures averaging 74.1°— more than six degrees above the norm. The heat really does come in waves west of the mountains: the general pattern is four very warm days, after which the marine layer moves in and the weather turns gray and cool for a couple of days, followed by gradual or in some cases sudden warming as another wave breaks. In the summer of 1996, which was fairly typical, four of these waves visited us in July and August. Whenever I start to grumble about yet another boring sunny day or groan about how much water I'm pouring onto the garden, my wife reminds me of the "triple H" weather we left behind back East: hazy, hot, and humid. This deadly summertime combination is extremely, blessedly, rare in the Northwest.

We notice heat waves west of the mountains more, not only because high temperatures are relatively uncommon, but because air conditioning is too. When it hits 90°, we swelter together. The thermometer inside my house read 82° at ten o'clock at night on July 14, 1996, during a weekend of record-breaking heat. The sun, which we crave all winter long, seems to mock us as it descends ever so slowly on those long, long summer days. At some point in late July or August we think about rain and can't quite remember the last time any fell. The infinite powder blue overhead looks as if it had never produced a cloud in its life and never will again, as if it clean forgot how. The only splash of water comes from lawn sprinklers. Beyond the irrigated perimeter, the earth is brown, hard, and dry. The light at midday is as dazzling and pale as it is in Arizona. The air is calm save for afternoon breezes. We weather nuts get a little disgusted with this endless meteorological tranquillity. "I'm always kind of depressed when it stops raining," an atmospheric researcher confessed to a *Seattle Times* reporter recently. "The summer is actually quite monotonous."

This guy, I happen to know, is from California and grew up weather-starved. But I notice that the Northwest natives revel in the warmth. *Isn't this great?* they say, grinning; *isn't it about time we had some of this?* They know the heat and drought are temporary; they're storing up.

The natives also know that summer does not automatically mean heat and drought. Cool drizzly weather does on occasion linger during July or August—or, worse, during July *and*

August. Summer rain doesn't usually amount to much (the wettest July in Seattle, recorded in 1983, brought only 2.39 inches of rain), but the gray is dispiriting. Gardens refuse to grow; flowers rot; molds and mildews flourish. These are the seasons that put everyone in a bad mood.

These cool cloudy summers are the exception—occurring only once every three or four years, according to local lore. In a "normal" summer in the Pacific Northwest, low rainfall and warm temperatures bake moisture out of earth and plants; by August, forest fire becomes a serious danger, especially in the arid eastern region. Classic fire weather is prolonged drought followed by a heat wave with low humidities and a steady east wind. Such conditions occurred early in September 1902, when more than 110 fires raged in western Oregon and Washington, destroying an estimated $13 million worth of property. According to Northwest writer Stewart Holbrook's 1945 book *Burning an Empire,* at the height of the blaze, 700,000 acres were burning simultaneously and at night the glow of flame could be seen from the vicinity of Bellingham nearly all the way down to Eugene. "Darkest Day in the History of Seattle," a local newspaper declared after a smoke-black sky forced residents to turn lights on during the day. A sooty gray "snow" of cinders fell half an inch deep on Portland. A reporter for the *Columbian* weekly newspaper wrote of the destruction in southwestern Washington: "What a week ago was the beautiful valley of the Lewis River is now a hot and silent valley of death, spotted with the blackened bodies of both man and beast." It was, as Holbrook put it, "the most tremendous series of forest fires that white men ever saw west of the Cascade mountains."

Even more ferociously destructive was the so-called Tillamook Burn of August 1933. The fire began on the afternoon

of August 14, a hot, dry day with winds blowing smartly out
of the northeast—the ideal setup for a conflagration. A logging crew inadvertently ignited the blaze: some men were
hauling a log, and the friction of a cable rubbing against a
dry stump was enough to get a fire going. Once lit, it spread
rapidly through the woods. After several days, firefighters
believed they had the blaze under control, but they were
wrong. Eleven days after the thing started, it erupted again
and went crazy. Holbrook, who witnessed the fire, put this
florid but arresting description of its climax in *Burning an
Empire:* "The wind over the fire rose to a gale, almost to a
hurricane, as the wind always does when such a fire is burning.
The noise was greater than the sea ever made on the wild
Oregon shore; it roared and thundered and was marked by
the deep booming of ancient firs, still untouched by flame,
as the gale uprooted and sent them crashing down. . . . For
forty miles along the Pacific shore smoke and fire rolled out
over the ocean, carrying burning twigs, branches, even whole
treetops; and incoming tides showed how much of Oregon
had been blown to sea. The tides piled black debris two feet
deep for miles along the beaches." In a single twenty-four-hour
period, from August 24 to 25, 270,000 acres were consumed.
The smoke rose nearly eight miles into the atmosphere. In
total, the Tillamook Burn blackened some 311,000 acres,
destroying 12.5 billion board feet of timber—not just weedy
second growth but, as Holbrook wrote, ancient Douglas firs
"that had been 400 years in the making. It was wiped out
in a few seething hours which Oregon will have reason to
remember well past the year 2000."

Weather ignited the blaze and weather helped end it:
on August 25, the wind shifted, a dense fog crept in from
the ocean, and the worst of the fire was over.

The Tillamook Burn was unique in this century for its explosiveness and for the age and size of the trees it consumed, but it was by no means an isolated event. Forest fires still burn in the Pacific Northwest every dry summer—in the past few decades we've had major burns in 1970, 1986, 1987, 1994, and 1996. In 1994, one of the worst years in recent memory, some 232,149 acres of public forest burned in Washington State and 240,194 burned in Oregon. By August of that year a pall of smoky haze dimmed most of the mountain ranges of the West, and on any given day a fire was burning out of control somewhere.

Just like the "good old days." I was disturbed to learn that our pioneer ancestors routinely ignited forest fires every summer as a quick, cheap way to clear the land. One William Phillips of Clackamas County, Oregon, reported that when he arrived in 1846 the land was "almost perfect in all its wildness. . . . No fires had run in these forests for hundreds of years, the Indians being careful not to let the fire get out, lest the grass should be burned from their horses. . . . But early in the summer of 1847, when the immigrants began to arrive, fires got started in the forests. . . . Whole forests of red and yellow fir, of the giant arbor vitae, and of hemlock and tamarack were destroyed by these raging fires. Millions of acres were burned over and killed." The assumption back then was that the forest was infinite, while time and labor were in short supply. Now that we know better, only the insane and the criminal deliberately start forest fires. The rest of the conflagrations begin by "accident"—human carelessness and acts of God, along with the calculated risks that logging companies take when they operate during the dry season. But accident is enough, especially when combined with warm dry weather. Unless our climate alters radically or our forests all give way to lawn-sprinklered subdivisions, fire weather will remain a dangerous, unpredictable element of summer in the Northwest.

If June is often our cruelest month, September can be the kindest—warm, dry, golden, calm. The region has enjoyed so many of these balmy Septembers in recent years—twelve in a row, by some counts, from the early 1980s through the mid-1990s—that residents have come to take them for granted. September, in local lore, is the best of summer, with only shortening days to warn of the approach of autumn. And so it comes as something of a shock to learn that fine Septembers are something of a climatic anomaly. As Clifford Mass, professor of atmospheric sciences at the University of Washington, explains, the recent run of superb Septembers may have been the result of an unusually persistent El Niño— a recurrent warming of the equatorial Pacific that affects weather worldwide (see Chapter Four). In the Northwest El Niño is usually associated with winters that are warmer and drier than normal, but it may well bring us glorious Septembers as well. Current conditions certainly seem to bear this out: the winter of 1995–96 was the first in several years in which El Niño subsided, and it was also one of the wettest on record in much of the region. The September that followed brought cool temperatures and 1.85 inches of rain to Seattle—which felt like a deluge to folks accustomed to a string of Tuscan Septembers, but was in fact just about normal for the month.

Glancing back through my weather journal, I see that the rain commenced on the evening of September 2 in "a brief slug-producing shower" and hung on for the better part of two weeks. By September 19, I was sounding real cranky:

No matter what the forecast gurus say, we seem to
get some rain just about every day. Yesterday: The
much-heralded clearing never came; in fact, by noon
it had begun to sprinkle (maybe 20 minutes of sun
in midmorning), and it sprinkled and drizzled and
rained and misted and drizzled all day long and into
the evening. President Clinton, delivering a campaign
speech at Pike Place Market, got wet for the first time
in five years of visiting Seattle. A real fall rainy day—
in the upper 50s, chill, and wet. Misty and damp this
morning, but the dense fog of dawn has lifted somewhat; still gray. Supposed to get partly sunny by late
afternoon, then clouds roll back in; rain tomorrow;
some clearing Saturday; more rain arrives by Monday.
Or something like that. The only trouble with forecasts like these is that it often forgets to clear at all
and we just go from gloom to gloom to dripping. Now
we seem to be in a pattern where the "chance of rain
late in the day" forecast means rain followed by light
rain followed by drizzle. Cool and raw with intermittent wet seems to be the order of the day.

In truth, I really didn't have anything to grouse about: as
recently as 1978, nearly 6 inches of rain fell on Sea-Tac airport in September.

"People don't have any memory, meteorologically," weather
historian David Ludlum reminds us. Northwesterners who
lived through the damp, chill Septembers of yesteryear have
forgotten them. Recent arrivals like me never knew them.
And so, when September 1996 turned out cool and moist, we
all set up a hue and cry as if it was the end of the world. In
fact, it was only the end of summer.

Chapter Three

"Don't believe
all that is said
about Oregon"

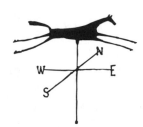

SETTLING IN WITH
THE WEATHER

EVEN AFTER BEING DISCOVERED multiple times—overland and by sea; from the south, west, and east; by Spanish, English, and American explorers—the Pacific Northwest remained shrouded in damp gray mystery. Exploring parties had glimpsed (or in some cases endured) its coastal perimeter and the great rivers that slashed through mountain and plain, but little was known of the land beyond the water. And those few scraps of knowledge did not excite or entice the nineteenth-century imagination. The trees were too big, the forests too dark, the mountains too steep and too abundant, the rivers too turbulent, and the climate, the already notoriously awful climate, was too impossibly wet. Lewis and Clark had confirmed reports and rumors stretching back two and a half centuries: *It really did rain all the time.* If anything, the captains extended and deepened the region's dank and dismal reputation. Not only did they keep a vividly detailed accounting of the ceaseless rain and wind, but they added unpleasant new discoveries such as vicious fleas, dishonest Indians, and a forbidding landscape divided between dripping black forest in the west and bleak shadeless desert in the east.

It's difficult to comprehend how the rain-soaked journals of Lewis and Clark could inspire in anyone a lifelong passion for Oregon, but such was the case with a New England schoolmaster named Hall Jackson Kelley. Back in 1817, Kelley, who was something of a visionary and something of a lunatic, read the journals and latched onto the one favorable thing that the captains had to say about the region—that a river they called Multnomah (what we call the Willamette) was blessed with a fertile valley reminiscent of Lewis's beloved Shenandoah country back in old Virginia. This river country was, wrote Lewis, "the only desireable situation for a settlement which I have seen on the West side of the Rocky mountains." Lewis tossed off this remark as little more than an aside while the Corps of Discovery was beating its way out of the Pacific Northwest as fast as boats would carry them up the Columbia, but it fired Kelley's imagination with a burning passion: he was going to see Oregon settled by Christian Americans, or he would die trying.

Kelley was a peculiar man by every account; he opened a chapter in one of his numerous books with the assertion "I am Hall J. Kelley; that is my name. . . . *Stupid, ignorant and crazy;* I have often been spoken of in this way." But he set about accomplishing his mission with a bumbling zeal. An almost total ignorance of the promised land of Oregon was no barrier, for Kelley invented and embroidered as he propagandized. "Kelley's capacity for wonder was unlimited," wrote Robert Cantwell in *The Hidden Northwest*. "By some instinct he knew that the reports of a wholly inhospitable wilderness in the Northwest must be false, and in default of firsthand information he decided that Oregon was, on the contrary, a land of fertile valleys, beautiful mountains, rushing rivers and a benign climate." "Benign climate" is putting it mildly. Before he ever set foot on Oregon soil, breathed a lungful of its air, or felt a drop of its rain, Kelley rhapsodized thus about the region's weather in a tract entitled *A Geographical Sketch of that Part of North America Called Oregon* (published in Boston in 1830), a marvel of invention, fantasy, and wishful thinking—the kind of prose that real estate and travel agents specialize in:

> We are fully justified in the general remark, that no
> portion of the globe presents a more fruitful soil, or
> a milder climate, or equal facilities for carrying into
> effect the great purposes of a free and enlightened
> nation. . . . Providence in this gift, especially, has made
> Oregon the most favoured spot of His beneficence.
> If any part of this country is more salubrious in cli-
> mate than another, it is the great plains at the foot of
> the mountains. These plains are less subject to rains;
> more remote from the sea, and better sheltered by
> stupendous mountains. Nevertheless it is warmer on
> the coast. The many lofty mountains situated in a high
> latitude, reflecting from their southern declivities the
> rays of the sun with the great effect, and protecting
> the country from the cold winds of the North, and
> from the violence of the storms of the Southeast,
> greatly meliorate the atmosphere, and produce that

surprising difference between the climates on the
western and eastern sides of the American Continent.

As for the fabled rains, Kelley admitted their existence but dismissed them as a trifling matter: "In the neighborhood of the
mouth of the Columbia, rains are frequent in the winter. They
commence with the South-east winds about the first of December,
and terminate the last of February, when benign Spring has made
some advance, 'the singing of birds has come,' and Nature dresses
again in her loveliest garb. In April, a mild summer heat obtains,
shrubbery is in blossom, and vegetation proceeds briskly. In June
all kinds of mild fruit are ripened, and weather, delightfully
pleasant, succeeds."

The part about the rains terminating the last of February
would have come as a surprise to Lewis and Clark, who continued to get drenched on a daily basis well into April. But no
matter. Kelley may have been a wild-eyed visionary with a pen-
chant for grandiose distortion ("stupid, ignorant and crazy"), but
at the heart of his ravings there was a shrewd political agenda: to
secure Oregon for the burgeoning United States. Oregon, which
in those days encompassed the entire Pacific Northwest, had been
in political limbo ever since the end of the War of 1812. In nego-
tiating the Treaty of Ghent, which ended the war in 1818, Britain
and America were unable to determine which side had a better
claim to the region, so they agreed to leave it as "free and open"
country under their joint jurisdiction—sort of a demilitarized
no-man's land. The British swiftly made their presence felt through
the venerable Hudson's Bay Company, which took over the rich
fur trade and set up a network of fortified trading posts, but that
was about as far as they wanted to go; permanent agricultural

colonies of homesteading families were not part of the British game plan. That's where Hall Kelley came in. Kelley knew that the presence of substantial numbers of American settlers would bolster America's claim on the Oregon country. "England is desirous of possessing the whole country, with all its invaluable privileges," he all but ranted in the concluding section of *Geographical Sketch*. "It is not a doubtful hypothesis, that unless our legitimate rights on the waters and in the territory of Oregon, are protected by planting a colony in it, or by other means no less effectual; they will in a few years more, become entirely lost to our merchants, or to the benefits of our country." Let this earthly paradise of "fruitful soil" and "salubrious climate" slip through American fingers? Never! Kelley's campaign, launched under the banner of his newly founded American Society for Encouraging the Settlement of the Oregon Territory, was one of the first herald blasts of Manifest Destiny.

In Kelley's overheated prose, weather itself became a political weapon. Oregon's miraculous mildness was going to draw settlers like a magnet, and once a sufficient number of them arrived (Kelley specifies "three thousand of the active sons of American freedom"), the region would fall into America's hands like a heavy ripe apple. He was not alone in using weather to whip up Oregon fever. Missouri Senator Lewis F. Linn, for example, rhapsodized in 1838 about Oregon's almost "tropical" climate. Pamphlets and rumors about the land without a winter began circulating back to chilblained New England and the mercurial Midwest. Oregon was the place.

Kelley himself did eventually make it out here, embarking from Boston in the autumn of 1832 and suffering a series of bizarre misadventures that took him down to New Orleans and Mexico City, across the deserts of Arizona, and up into Spanish-controlled northern California, where his mountain men companions rounded up and stole a herd of horses. By the time he reached Oregon Territory more than two years later, Kelley was half dead and wanted as an accomplice horse thief. Treated as a pariah by the officers of the Hudson's Bay Company headquarters at Fort Vancouver, he lived through one marvelously mild North-west winter in an isolated shack formerly used for fish cleaning. Only three times during the glorious winter did snow cover the ground, and it remained but briefly. A cold snap in February passed as quickly as it came. Kelley recorded in awe that "for a few hours houses, trees and fields sparkled with an icy covering." It was indeed the promised land, but he could not secure a toe-hold on it. In the spring he left, sailing to Hawaii and eventually returning empty-handed to Boston.

For years afterward Kelley petitioned the U.S. government for some kind of reward or recognition for the suffering and hard work he had devoted to the cause of Oregon—but to no avail. As one historian wrote, he "never succeeded, during thirty years of trying, in convincing Congress or the nation that his Oregon efforts were worth a grant of land to help out his old age."

The sole reward Kelley received was vindication, for of course his dream of an Oregon thickly settled by American farmers came swiftly and triumphantly true. People trickled in starting in the 1830s—missionaries, visionaries, French trappers with Native American wives. Then in the 1840s, as Oregon fever swept the nation, they came in a flood. An estimated 280,000 people set out westward along the fabled Oregon Trail between 1845 and 1859.

Some 30,000 of them died along the way. Many more turned south at the Raft River beyond Fort Hall and headed down to California. But a substantial number (some 53,000 between 1840 and 1860) ended their journey just where Hall J. Kelley hoped they would, in Oregon Territory. Farmers for the most part, they settled the Willamette River valley first—Lewis and Clark's fabled Multnomah—because large stretches of the land were already open and grassy and ready to be plowed; in fact, the area looked as if it had *already* been farmed. "The whole of the River is very beautiful and rich Country and happy Climate," noted British fur trader and explorer David Thompson. "The Paradise of farmers," another early visitor raved. "The whole country was a natural park," commented one pioneer upon arrival; "it seem[ed] to me like dream land." The grassy plains of central Whidbey Island and a few treeless sections bordering Puget Sound also attracted settlers for the same reason. The first farmers wisely steered clear of the towering forests, which would require decades to clear for plowing.

These pioneers, most of whom came from the Midwest, assumed they would grow corn, just as they did back home in Ohio, Missouri, or Illinois—but they soon discovered that corn did not prosper in the Northwest. The summer was too dry and the nights too cool to yield a decent crop. Instead, wheat became the staple of the Northwest farms, with 160,000 bushels produced in Oregon country in 1846. Wheat was so common in the Willamette Valley that the provisional government made it the territory's legal tender at a dollar a bushel.

Settlers who had come to Oregon expressly for the much-touted climate were in for something of a shock, especially if they arrived during the rainy season, as many did. One Dr. John Scouler compared the "incessant" rains he experienced in Oregon from 1824 to 1826 to equatorial downpours. "The climate I consider good was it not for the rains of winter which last from three to six months," wrote W. C. Dement from Oregon City to his mother back in Georgetown in July 1845. Dement added proudly that his farm had yielded a good crop of wheat, oats, and potatoes. "We may now call ourselves through, they say," wrote Amelia Stewart Knight of her family's completion of the Oregon Trail in 1853, "and here we are in Oregon, making our camp in an ugly bottom, with no home, except our wagons and tent, it is drizzling and the weather looks dark and gloomy."

Pioneer W. S. Gilliam offered a more extensive and dramatic account of the weather that greeted him and his parents upon their arrival in Oregon Territory in November 1844, some eight and a half months after departing from their home in western Missouri: "Before we reached the Cascade Falls the gates of heaven seemed to have opened and the rain came down in torrents. . . . Enduring hunger, drenching rains and traveling over the worst roads that I ever saw we reached Vancouver early in December. In taking a retrospect of my life I regard this trip from the Dalles to Vancouver as the severest hardship that it was ever my lot to endure. For days and nights my clothes were never dry." Lucie Fulton Isaacs, though only six in 1847 when her family emigrated from St. Joseph, Missouri, to a claim in Yamhill County, Oregon, never forgot her first experience of a wet Northwest winter: "Oh! how it did rain that first winter, and mother often had tears in her eyes, and child though I was I think I realized something of the sick longing she had for her old home."

It's fitting, given its rainy reputation, that the city of Seattle should have been founded on a day of wretched weather. The founding fathers and mothers who made up the Denny party— twelve adults and twelve children in all—left Illinois in the spring of 1851 and arrived in Portland 108 days later. Like most pioneers of the time, they had intended to find claims in the Willamette, but someone told them about Puget Sound and at some point they set their hearts on settling there instead. David T. Denny and a small exploring party reconnoitered the region in September, and the rest of the folks sailed up from Portland in mid-November on a schooner called the *Exact*. They disembarked near Alki Point in what is today West Seattle. The story goes that when they gathered on the shore, David Denny, emerging from the bushes, met them with this hearty greeting: "I am mighty glad to see you folks, for the skunks have eaten all my grub." That was the only gladness any of them felt that day. Historian and University of Washington luminary Edmond S. Meany conjured up the grim scene in his *History of the State of Washington:* "A dreary autumn rain was falling. There was no shelter. The schooner continued on to Olympia. The colony was alone. . . . Arthur A. Denny [David's older brother] turned to his friend and said: 'Low, white women are scarce in these parts. We had better take care of what we have.' He found his own wife sitting on a log, her back against a tree. In her arms was a babe but a few weeks old. She was weeping. 'Come, come, wife, this is no way to begin pioneering.' 'Oh, you promised when we left Illinois that we would not settle in a wilderness. Now see where we are.' The foundation of Seattle was laid in a mother's tears." Rain and tears. Arthur Denny reported in his own history of the city that the rain they encountered that first day continued, "falling more or less every day, but we did not regard it with much concern and seldom lost any time on that account." How reassuring that the entrenched Seattle custom of refusing to break for rain dates back to the city's earliest days. Denny added at the end of his book that the mildness of that winter was some consolation for the wetness: "We had but little snow and no freezing to speak of, and ice not more than half an inch in thickness."

The following winter, however, was far more severe—"one of our coldest," wrote Denny, with "a twelve-inch snow on [Elliott Bay]. . . . The snow remained on the ground two or three weeks. Ice formed on the mud flats and mouth of the [Duwamish] river, and floated back and forth with the tide so as to seriously interfere with boats and canoes crossing the bay." Ezra Meeker, a native of Ohio who arrived via the Oregon Trail at the start of this severe winter season of 1852–53, confirmed Denny's recollections of deep and enduring snow. Like thousands of other pioneers, Meeker traveled out to Oregon in large part because of the fabled climate, and he spoke for many when he described the depression that hit when he realized just how awful winter in the Northwest could be:

> As a young man of twenty-two with my young wife, I
> can truly say that it was the lure of climate that drew
> us to the Oregon country and brought the final deci-
> sion to undertake the memorable trip over the
> Oregon Trail. To say that we realized what that trip
> involved would not be ingenuous; but it proved to be
> an undertaking far more strenuous than we had
> counted on and I think such was the case with nearly
> all of the pioneers of that day. With two feet of snow

> falling within sixty days after arrival, our ideals as to
> climate vanished. Discouragement and discontent
> reigned supreme among the newly arrived immi-
> grants. I believe nine-tenths of them would have left
> the country immediately if they could, but they
> couldn't get away. . . .

Some who couldn't get away from the rotten weather eventually relocated to drier parts of the Northwest. W. S. Gilliam, the
Missouri transplant who recorded his wet discomfort upon
arriving in western Oregon, was among these émigrés from rain.
He wrote that by 1859, "we became disgusted with the long wet
dreary [Willamette] winters that coupled with the growing
shortage of the public pasturage caused us to sell and seek a
country with less winter rains and more public range." And so
they pulled up stakes and moved to Walla Walla, with a mean
annual rainfall of 19.5 inches.

It was during these pioneering years that the nicknames
"mossback" and "webfoot" began to be affixed to Northwesterners. As reports from settlers like Gilliam, the Dennys, and
Lucie Isaacs began to spread back East, the notion of a climatic
Eden in Oregon began to fade behind the high clouds of a new
weather mythology: *Rains all the time*. As Oregon historian
Richard Maxwell Brown wrote in his fascinating essay "Rainfall
and History: Perspectives on the Pacific Northwest," "By the
middle of the nineteenth century, with the American flag flying
over present Oregon and Washington, the image of oppressive
rainfall was as well established as the homes of pioneers from
Puget Sound to the Rogue River. Jokes began to circulate about
the persistent precipitation." The region has never succeeded in

shaking off those jokes (and with good reason, some would insist).

And yet the weather reports penned by the first settlers were not all gloom and drizzle. Many wrote with pleased surprise about the mildness of the winters, the early and gradual advent of spring—so unlike the sudden explosion of the season in the East and Midwest—and the moderate temperatures of summer. Ross Cox, not a settler but an employee of John Jacob Astor's ill-fated Pacific Fur Company, who lived in Astoria for five years (from 1812 to 1817) before sailing back to his native Dublin, included this discourse on the region's mildness in his popular *Adventures on the Columbia River* (published in two volumes in 1831): "The climate on the Columbia River, from its mouth to the rapids, is mild. The mercury seldom falls below the freezing point, and never rises above 80°. Westerly winds prevail during the spring and summer months, and are succeeded by northwesters, which blow pretty freshly during the autumn. . . ." Meeker marveled over the delights of his first Northwestern spring and the long growing season that followed: "The February sun of 1853 shone almost like midsummer. The clearing [around the cabin] grew almost as if by magic. We could not resist the temptation to begin planting, and before March was gone, the rows of peas, lettuce, and onions growing on the river bank could be seen from the cabin door. . . . Our spirits grew apace with the garden stuff and our dreams of the Oregon climate seemed to be realized; then when the later planting of hardy vegetables grew all through the month of November, we were happy in the thought we had made no mistake in choosing Oregon country for our future home."

Meeker admitted that the Pacific Northwest did not have "an ideal climate made to order," but he "boldly" proclaimed that it is "a beautiful climate and healthy without comparison." And he summed up its virtues in a crescendo of praise: "The prevailing winds from off the wide expanse of the Pacific Ocean, the oft cleansing of the atmosphere (washing, shall I say?) from frequent rains, the refreshing cool nights that invariably appear as old Sol disappears, the absence of sweltering, enervating heat in summer and lurking malarial germs, all combine to provide surroundings to invigorate the system."

Newspaperman Charles Prosch, an émigré from New York who founded the *Puget Sound Herald* after settling in Steilacoom in 1858, proclaimed the climate of the Puget Sound region the very finest in the world, even during the rainy season: "It was now near the end of February," he wrote in *Reminiscences of Washington Territory*, "and the sun never shone upon a lovelier day, in Italy or elsewhere, than that on which I quit the vessel for my new home. Nor was this charming weather confined to one or two days; weeks and months elapsed before it changed, and then for three or four days only. During the last week in June refreshing rains visited us, but the sky again cleared within a week, and we had no more rain until November. Thus I found the climate here much better than that of San Francisco, which some years before I thought was incomparably superior to that of the Atlantic states. This agreeable feature of Puget Sound had much to do with making me and mine contented in our new home."

Even more glowing reports of the weather appeared in Theodore Winthrop's florid but fascinating volume *The Canoe and the Saddle*. A great-great-great-great-grandson of John Winthrop, the first governor of the Massachusetts Bay Colony, and a fresh graduate of Yale, Theodore Winthrop was the quintessential Yankee in search of adventure, novelty, and something grand and original to write about. He arrived in Oregon Territory in the summer of 1853 and commenced his adventures by promptly contracting smallpox, then ravaging the native tribes. Once he recovered, he embarked on a lightning-fast trek through the region by canoe and horseback—whence came the title of his book. Winthrop's journey began up in Victoria toward summer's end (usually the time of the year's finest weather), and in under two weeks he covered some 320 miles—down into Puget Sound, up onto the snowfields of Mount Rainier (one of whose glaciers is named for him), over the Cascades, down into Yakima and its broad valley, and across the plains to the Columbia River. Privileged but not the least bit jaded, Winthrop swallowed the grandeur and variety of Northwest scenery in huge greedy gulps. The book Winthrop composed three years after returning to his home on tepid, rolling Staten Island fairly glowed with enthusiastic ardor. Yes, his prose is mannered and at times overwrought, but Winthrop sweeps us along with him in his passion for Northwest landscape, topography, vegetation, and, of course, weather. (He was far less enthralled with the native peoples, whom he portrayed for the most part as dirty, drunken, and disreputable buffoons.) Winthrop composed a virtual prose symphony on the theme of Storm Clouds Parting Over the Cascade Mountains:

> By the hearty aid of noon, the Cascades put their
> shoulders to the clouds, lifted them and cut them to
> pieces with their peaks, so that the wind could come
> in, like a charge of cavalry, and annihilate the broken

phalanxes. Mount Adams, Tacoma [the name he used
for Mount Rainier] the Less, was the first object to
cleave the darkness. I looked westward, and saw a
sunlit mass of white, high up among the black clouds,
and baseless but for them. It would have seemed itself
a cloud, but, while the dark volumes were heaving and
shifting about it, this was permanent. While I looked,
the mountain and the sun became evident victors; the
glooms fell away, were scattered and scourged into
nothingness, and the snow-peak stood forth majestic,
the sole arbiter of this realm.

In one notable passage, Winthrop prophesied rhapsodically
that the combined influence of "great mountains" and a climate
"where being is bliss" would engender a new race of human
beings in the Pacific Northwest. The people of Oregon were, in
Winthrop's mind, destined to elaborate "new systems of thought
and life" and give the "American Idea" its ultimate expression.
This is a fairly tall order. But Winthrop was clearly intoxicated by
what he describes as "the unapproachable glory of an Oregon
summer sky." I know how he felt. There *is* something almost
supernatural about the finest summer weather here. And back in
1853, before clear-cuts and suburban sprawl had marred the
landscape, it must have been like paradise itself. Winthrop had a
touch of the transcendentalist in him—and a touch of the wide-
eyed American boy on a lark. (And of course he had very good
luck and good timing meteorologically. Had he stayed on into
November, his fervor might have cooled down a bit.)

Winthrop was transformed by his sojourn amid our mountains, rivers, sounds, and clear summer skies. As he wrote with
Thoreavian rapture at the conclusion of his book: "And in all that

period while I was so near to Nature, the great lessons of the wilderness deepened into my heart day by day, the hedges of conventionalism withered away from my horizon, and all the pedantries of scholastic thought perished out of my mind forever." Like many an aspiring writer, Theodore Winthrop died unrecognized, his Northwest travelogue and his five novels all rejected by the publishers of his day. Death brought him the fame that had eluded him during his lifetime: Winthrop was the first Union officer killed in the Civil War, and the Northern press instantly made him a hero in 1861. At last his books, including *The Canoe and the Saddle,* found publishers. The success of that volume helped spread the word that there was more to the Northwest climate than incessant rain.

A more measured and realistic assessment of the region's weather appeared in James Gilchrist Swan's absorbing book *The Northwest Coast.* Swan, a middle-aged Massachusetts man with a wife, two young children, and a good job in Boston outfitting sailing ships, left it all behind in 1850 to join the westward stampede of the California gold rush. He never did pan for gold, though he made it out to the Sacramento mining camps as the purser aboard a river steamer. Living in the West seems to have made Swan even more restless. He took a job on a trading schooner bound for Hawaii, returned to San Francisco's roaring waterfront to work as a clerk in a ship-outfitting business, and promptly got the travel itch again. Late in 1852, at the invitation of a new friend, Swan decided to sail up the coast and see what the Pacific Northwest was all about. "I had always, from my earliest recollections, a strong desire to see the great River Columbia," he wrote by way of explanation. His destination was actually not the Columbia but a coastal indent just north of the river called Shoalwater Bay (now Willapa Bay), a soggy beach-head that supported a straggling settlement of a dozen white homesteaders and oystermen and a scattering of migrants from the Chinook and Chehalis tribes. As Ivan Doig wrote in *Winter Brothers,* his wonderful volume of meditations on Swan's life and journal, "Put at its more generous, this colony on the eastern shore of Shoalwater Bay in the early 1850s . . . amounted more to an episode of prolonged beachcombing than a serious effort at enterprise." But it was here Swan stuck, at least for three years.

Like the Denny party of the previous year, Swan had the mis-fortune of arriving in November—and of course it was storming. A gale kicked up as the ship he was on reached the latitude of the Columbia, and by November 24 the wind had raised the sea into such a frenzy that it smashed the window of the ship's cabin. The entry into Shoalwater Bay was hair-raising: "The breakers were very high," Swan wrote, "and foamed, and roared, and dashed around us in the most terrific manner." Eventually he made it to shore, found shelter, and patched together a life. While at Shoal-water, Swan earned a scant income from the government as the assistant customs collector for the coast north of the Columbia, a post that left him plenty of time for wandering the shoreline, get-ting acquainted with the Indians, scrutinizing the land and sea and the weather that rolled over them, drinking, and writing. The result of the latter was *The Northwest Coast,* published in 1857. The book, which rambles genially over a good deal of varied ter-rain, is perhaps most noteworthy for its humane, unsensational depictions of native peoples—as Doig put it, Swan had a "rare knack of looking at the coastal Indians as flesh and blood rather than the frontier's tribal rubble." But Swan also had the knack of conveying the *feel* of the wild environment he had come to dwell in, and the book includes some valuable observations and musings on the weather of Washington's coast. Like many a newcomer, Swan was struck by the fact that so northerly a region should have such mild winters. "I have never known excessive cold weather to continue longer than twelve or fourteen days," he wrote, "when the wind will return to the south, and warm rain brings on a general thaw. . . . It is these facts with respect to the climate that make a residence in either Oregon or Washington Territories so desirable; and the remarkable fact should not be lost sight of, that, although Washington Territory is in the same latitude as Nova Scotia, yet the climate is as mild in winter as Pennsylvania. . . ." Swan was careful to qualify this encomium by explaining that even though Oregon and Washington winters are mild, "still it must not be supposed that a winter's residence in either territory is attended with the delights of a tropical climate"—a statement that even the most fervid Northwest partisan would not dispute. As he added, however, delights do prevail in summer, when the temperature "rarely exceeds 80°" (although he noted that he had seen it climb as high as 95° for short periods).

As for precipitation, Swan tackled—and debunked—the rains-all-the-time mythology: "During the winter rain falls in the most incredible quantities, but it does not, as has been asserted, rain without intermission. A storm will commence which will last a week, some days raining violently, and accompanied with heavy gales of wind. These blows will last perhaps twenty-four or forty-eight hours, when it will lull, and the rain subsides into a gentle shower, or mere mist and fog; then perhaps it will clear off, with eight or ten days of fine, clear weather."

It wasn't the rain that got to him, he confessed, but the combination of rain and winter dark: "From the high latitude of Shoalwater Bay, the days are very short, and but little out-door work can be done, and the settler finds it a difficult task to pass off the long, stormy nights, unless with the aid of books or some useful in-door employment." The saving grace is the early advent of spring. As Swan recorded with a naturalist's precision: "On the 10th day of March, 1853, while making a botanical collection, I gathered the blossoms of the wild raspberry (Rubus spectablis), the fruit of which is ripe in June, the wild strawberry, the Trillium (Dikentra formosa), and various other small flowers; while in the month of my arrival, December, 1852, I collected and preserved the blossoms of the Salal (Gaultheria Shallon)." And he concluded, with newly kindled Northwest chauvinism: "What part of the country east of the Rocky Mountains, in the latitude of 46° north, can be shown where flowers bloom from March to December?"

Swan, during his years on the Northwest coast at Shoalwater and later at Port Townsend and Neah Bay, got used to the "incredible quantities" of the winter rains and even came to rely on them. Other settlers developed a healthy appreciation, or even a fondness, for the seasonal downpours. Oregon pioneer Peter H. Burnett wrote in a letter in 1844 that the winter rains were "much less troublesome" than he had anticipated and that in fact he much preferred Oregon's "gentle showers" and "drizzling rains" to the gully-washers that afflicted his native Missouri. Washington newspaper publisher Charles Prosch told of a "genial doctor named Price" who was forced to give up his Steilacoom practice in the early 1860s because "the population was too sparse and the climate too healthy to afford him a livelihood"; so he went to southern California and endured three years "in that sunny clime—three years of uninterrupted drouth." Finally, unable to stand the sun any longer, Dr. Price returned to Olympia, where Prosch found him standing outside with his hat off, his face turned reverently to the dripping sky as he exclaimed joyously: "Thank God, I am once more in a country where it rains!" The author of a history of Benton County, Oregon, boasted of the "remarkable regularity" of the rainy season as "the foundation of the agricultural wealth" of his glorious state. Another imaginative early settler, studying his atlas, noticed that Oregon occupied "precisely the same parallels of latitude" as France and exactly the same geographic orientation—ocean to the west, continental landmass to the east—and from this concluded that the climate, rain and all, was optimal, since the French climate "has long since and universally been acknowledged one of the finest on the globe."

Chauvinistic, yes, but perhaps not quite as outlandish as it sounds. Consider the recent success of Oregon grape growers and wine-makers in producing excellent wines from the classic French grape varieties.

Rain in one guise or another dominated the meteorological musings of the pioneers who settled between the western flanks of the Cascades and the Pacific Ocean. But those who staked their claims east of the mountains had very different climatic preoccupations. The aridity of the terrain in the Cascade rain shadow came as a shock to many an Oregon-bound pioneer: just when they thought they were approaching the precincts of paradise, the land seemed to die all around them into a stark, blazing, treeless desert. As one early settler recalled from his journey out to Oregon, "The sagebrush lands through which we passed in 1843 appeared to be worthless, not only because of the apparent sterility of the soil, but for the want of water." "Sad must be the disappointment of the emigrants," wrote Theodore Winthrop in a letter to his mother, "who have heard of the beauty of the country, on arriving there in the autumn, when every green thing is parched, themselves wayworn, their wealth of cattle become poverty,—half starved and almost hopeless." Winthrop himself found the "desolate and wild" territory around The Dalles "a region like the Valley of Death, rugged, bleak, and severe. A tragical valley, where the fiery forces of Nature, impotent to attain majestic combination, and build monuments of peace, had fallen into despairs and ugly warfare."

Given the barrenness of the landscape, the newcomers assumed that the Inland Empire, as the interior region came to be known, was unsuitable for farming. As Archibald McDonald of the Hudson's Bay Company reported back to his superiors, "the intense heat and constant drought of the summer are much against cultivation in the interior of the Columbia." And indeed there were crop failures due to drought at the Hudson's Bay Company farms in eastern Washington in 1839 and again in 1840. Meeker reported that in the mid-1850s, when he emigrated to the Northwest, the prevailing belief among settlers was that the "wide expanse of arid land of the eastern section" would never become an "agricultural country."

Too dry to farm, but not too dry to graze cattle. For farmers who had grown weary of the damp Willamette winters, ranching in the open, sunny plains across the mountains looked like a "life of ease," as one would-be cattle baron put it, and a small migration eastward over the mountains commenced in the late 1850s. But once again, newcomers brought with them some serious misconceptions about the climate. They knew about the aridity of the rain shadow country, but they didn't realize that the moderating influence of the Pacific Ocean peters out east of the Cascades, allowing far greater variability in temperatures. Philip Cox was among these climatically deluded émigrés. In 1859 Cox left the Willamette with a group of buddies to try ranching near Walla Walla. "The young men made no provisions for winter," he wrote years later, "for they had the impression there was no winter in this region." How sorely mistaken they were, they and hundreds of others soon discovered. All through the Inland Empire, the winter of 1861–62 froze any lingering dreams of a life of ease. It had been a dry summer and autumn, with no appreciable precipitation falling in September, October, November, or much of December. But December 22 brought heavy snow, and from then on the snow was pretty much constant, piling up through April and remaining on the ground in shady places into June. When "the coldest weather and deepest snow ever known here was over," wrote Cox, "every one of the herd belonging to the four young men was dead, but one." Margaret Gilbreath wrote with horror of the wolves that attacked her family's starving herd that winter: "The sound of hundreds of frenzied cattle bawling will not soon be forgotten." Another Willamette transplant reported that the Columbia was "thoroughly frozen up" and only 10 percent of his stock made it through the winter. "We are so shut out from the world that we do not know what the world is doing," reported Walla Walla's newspaper, the *Washington Statesman,* on February 8, 1862. "We could indeed tell you more about the weather—that fruitful theme for everybody's tongue— but about that you know as well as we."

Guy Waring, a gently bred New Englander and Harvard grad- uate who emigrated out to the Okanogan with his wife and stepchildren in the 1880s, wrote that settlers had learned in time to brace for these occasional spells of frigid weather: "Winters, I had been told, were not generally severe in the Okanogan, although about once in a decade the settlers might expect what they called 'a cow killer'—an unusually cold spell which could generally be depended upon to play havoc with the cattle." R. A. Long, in the book he co-authored about the Oregon desert, con- firmed the ten-year cycle of "cow-killer" winters. Where he came from, he wrote, that kind of winter was "called an 'equalizer' and everyone started even again."

The winter of 1861–62 changed "the whole of this part of the country," one early Walla Walla settler wrote: with their stock wiped out, the would-be ranchers were forced to try their luck at farming. Agricultural luck, of course, hinged on soil and weather conditions. The farmers who fanned out into the Palouse country of southeastern Washington in the last decades of the nineteenth century hit the jackpot. In this region, millennia of wind have piled up soil into deep water-retentive seams known as loess, and enough rain generally falls (16 to 24 inches a year is the average) to grow grains without irrigation. As one settler wrote proudly after his first year of farming in the Palouse: "The summer was all that we could want it to be. I heartily enjoyed looking over the beautiful country, fresh from the hands of nature and unmarred by the hands of man. Everything seemed to smile. The country became endeared to me and I have never seriously thought of making any other place my home." The open undulating hillsides of the Palouse yielded almost miraculous crops of wheat; and barley, dry peas, lentils, and grass seed also prospered. For a while, early settlers had high hopes for apple growing as well, but a streak of severe winters in the 1890s froze out the orchards, and after that the farmers pretty much stuck to grains, especially wheat. Lentils, first grown here by vegetarian Seventh-Day Adventists, were also perfectly suited to the region's climate, and today some 90 percent of the U.S. lentil harvest originates in the eastern Palouse.

Farmers found the drier sections in the Columbia basin, where annual rainfall dwindles to 7 to 10 inches annually, more problematic. After the Civil War, homesteaders came pouring into the high desert country with big dreams and little idea of how to realize them. "They came from everywhere and knew nothing of the country," wrote Jackman and Long in *The Oregon Desert*. "They thought that 'rainfall follows the plow.' They were of every occupation. The only thing they had in common was ignorance of dry-land farming." Once they plowed the short grass and sagebrush under, what little moisture the land held evaporated and the dry soil blew away in the desert winds. Those who hung on quickly realized that irrigation was crucial to making a go of farming in the arid belt of Washington and Oregon. As Peter Burnett wrote of eastern Oregon in his "Recollections and Opinions of an Old Pioneer": "With plentiful irrigation, I think it quite probable that these lands in most places, might be rendered fruitful. Water is a great fertilizer and nothing but experiment can actually demonstrate how far these wilderness plains can be redeemed."

The results of early experiments were promising indeed. Magazine editor and children's author Kirk Munroe, writing in *Harper's Weekly* in 1894, described the wonderful transformation of desert into garden in eastern Washington after water was introduced to the region's deep volcanic soils: "While the North Yakima of today, containing a population of 4000 souls, is . . . a place of abundant waters, grass, trees, flowers and pleasant houses, only eight years have elapsed since its site was as barren a bit of sagebrush desert as existed in eastern Washington. The region of which it formed a part was a poor grazing country, in which often more cattle starved to death than grew fat, and for agricultural purposes it was considered worthless. Its lands could hardly be given away, and few persons were found so poor as to be willing to accept them. The valley of the Yakima was considered to be cursed by the hottest of suns, the bluest of skies, and a drought rarely broken between April and November." Then, in the mid-1880s, a miracle befell this godforsaken place: wherever seeds came in contact with even a trickle of water, they "sprang up with the vigor and rapidity of Jack's beanstalk." There ensued the inevitable rush to channel the waters of the Yakima River into canals and irrigation ditches. "With irrigation an accomplished fact," wrote Munroe, "the very heat, the unbroken droughts and cloudless skies that prevail east of the Cascade Mountains, and once combined to make the desert a desert, have become most potent agents of prosperity. Owing to them, forage crops may be cured at any time in the open air with absolute certainty. Grain knows neither blight, rust nor mildew. Melons and small fruits attain a luscious maturity rivaling that of California."

As historian David Lavender wrote in his book *Land of Giants,* irrigation made Yakima bloom "with cash crops more valuable than roses. North of Yakima, at Wenatchee, irrigation systems fostered by Jim Hill's Great Northern Railroad pushed the value of apple lands up toward a thousand dollars an acre." The Inland Empire was found to be the ideal apple country, yielding not only an abundant crop but one remarkable for the perfection, size, and color of its fruit. Commercial export of apples began in 1900, and within a decade Washington and Oregon had outpaced New York and Missouri as the nation's major apple-growing states.

In time, as the pioneers hung on and put down roots on both sides of the Cascades, they and their descendants grew accustomed to and even fond of the vagaries of Pacific Northwest weather. Farmers in the Willamette, the Nisqually basin, and the Palouse, as well as townsfolk in Portland, Olympia, and Walla Walla, realized soon enough that they did not reside "in a climate where being is bliss"—but neither were they sprouting webs between their toes or moss on their backs, as the sunbaked Californians had joked they would. West of the mountains, folks adapted to their rainy winters and balmy dry summers, while settlers in the arid east quickly figured out what they could and could not grow in their hot parched fields and made allowances for the occasional cow-killer winters. As Oregon and Washington became established territories and then states (Oregon in 1859, Washington in 1889), the Northwest climate, or rather climates, became an integral part of regional identity and even a source of pride, though it was a somewhat ironic, skeptical kind of pride. Historian Richard Maxwell Brown even articulated a Northwest "ideology of climate" that both explains and defends what the heavens typically bring us:

> 1. The Northwest rain, while abundant, is gentle and "does not generally inhibit outdoor work and activity."
>
> 2. The reason rainfall seems "excessive" is that "it is concentrated in only about one half (or less) of the year."
>
> 3. The payback for the rainy season is mild winter temperatures and "the delightfully dry and sunny but not excessively hot summer weather."
>
> 4. "The regularity and dependability of Pacific Northwest temperature and precipitation are such that—in stark contrast to other parts of the country—the crops never fail."
>
> 5. All of the above results in a climate that is "unexcelled for the personal health of the individual, who benefits in terms of comfort and longevity."

Each of us may amend this list depending on where we live and what our preferred weather conditions are. Brown's list, to my mind, has a certain defensive, apologetic tone—the unstated assumption being that the climate here is not *really* as bad as it's cracked up to be. But these days, the prevailing ideology of climate insists that it *is* dreadful here for much of the year; in fact, it's even *worse* than everyone believes. As newcomers continue to pour into the region in search of "quality of life," residents have launched a deliberate, calculated plan of climatic obfuscation designed to keep people away. Slugs and umbrellas are the region's mascots. Locals hiss at newcomers when they boast about dry pleasant summers, and they nod sagely when weather wimps complain about yet another gray rainy day. Recently I heard a local radio announcer chuckle over a *Newsweek* cover story about how "everyone" sooner or later wants to move to Seattle and then, in the next breath, launch into his own vengeful long-range weather forecast: "It's going to rain today, it's going to rain tomorrow, it's going to rain for the rest of your life." We've entered a kind of reverse booster phase meteorologically—not bliss, but hell; not health, but depression. We want the world to know that *Lewis and Clark were right:* "O! how horriable is the day"—damp, disagreeable, flea-ridden. Dear old Hall J. Kelley is no doubt rolling in his New England grave.

Autumn

As my first autumn in the Northwest loomed, a neighbor up the street informed me authoritatively that the rainy season commenced on October 4. A neighbor down the street shook his head and murmured, smiling, "Now you won't see the sun again until next June." The fellow who came to tinker with the furnace, upon learning we were new arrivals from the East, asked whether we had heard about the annual Seattle Rain Festival—"Starts in October, ends the day after July 4."

Folks certainly do make a big deal about the rain out here. Or perhaps I should say "The Rains." For elsewhere in the country they get rain, but here in the Pacific Northwest we receive the more grandiose plural version: The Rains. The Rains do come as something of a shock after a long droughty summer. As it turned out, my neighbor up the street was uncannily right—at least that year (1993): after one of the driest Septembers on record, it did in fact start raining on October 5 (okay, so she was off by a day) and kept on raining for the next two days. But my neighbor down the street, it turned out, was indulging in typical Seattle scare tactics: the sun reappeared on October 9, elevating temperatures to a record-breaking 75°. The Rains and the sun played cat and mouse for the duration of the autumn, sun hanging tough through mid-October, rain gaining the upper hand through most of November. Still, I found myself wondering what all the fuss was about. The fabled Rains were for the most part gentle, intermittent, nocturnal. And there were a couple of spells that autumn when the sky kept its face scrubbed clean of clouds and the sun shone brightly, blindingly, for five or six days running.

In succeeding autumns (all of which, I must confess, have been a good deal wetter than that first one), I've continued to ponder the mystery of our rainy season and the hoopla that surrounds it. Maybe the key word here is not *rainy* but *season:* we notice our rain more because of its concentration. In the East and Midwest, precipitation is fairly evenly distributed through the year, and in the Plains states rain tends to fall in the summer, when farmers need it most. But here in the Northwest, almost all the rain comes down in the fall and winter, when nobody needs it except slugs and mushrooms. And our rains do often commence abruptly: one day, with barely an overture, the sky unfurls its curtains and the show begins. When I spoke to atmospheric scientist Cliff Mass, I told him about my neighbor's claim that the rainy season always started on October 4, expecting him to laugh it away as folklore. Instead, he gave me the scientific fine-tuning: "The probability of precipitation increases rapidly in October. The stormy period here is from November 10 through the end of February, with the last two weeks of November being the stormiest. The real heavy stuff is over by February."

I'm one of those people who both dread and eagerly antici-pate the "heavy stuff." Come mid-October, I'm spending far too much time snagging weather links on the Internet, squinting at radar updates, and gazing southwestward to see what's blowing up the Sound. In October 1996 I nearly went mad with frustration. After a damp September, the heavenly faucet screwed itself shut. Yes, we got the obligatory down-pour on October 4 (actually, it started the day before—a tenth of an inch or so, in that typical fitful Northwest pattern of a brief downpour followed by drizzle followed by mist fol-

lowed by congealing wet air followed by more drizzle). But
by October 6, the skies had cleared and it turned fair and
warm. And stayed that way. October 9 brought record-
breaking heat—79° in Seattle! While everyone else was
basking and exulting, I was fretting: too warm, too dry,
wasn't it "supposed" to be raining by now? By October 17
I had finally relaxed a bit: "What a fabulous day weatherwise,"
I crowed to my journal. "The wind really kicked up and blew
like crazy midmorning. Then it started to sprinkle, whereupon the wind settled down. Period of light rain fell through
most of midday. Then around 4:30 or 5 P.M. the heavy rain
settled in, wind whipped up and it rained hard, off and on,
until around 10 or 11 P.M. I know just how heavy that rain
got because I was out coaching soccer practice in it: hard and
cold—'Midwest rain,' one of the other parents said. 'This is
ridiculous' was the general consensus, though I think everyone was secretly enjoying it as much as I was. Total rain about
a half inch, maybe a bit more. Raw and cold. Mountains are
out just barely now, and there is quite a bit of snow on them."

It took just four days for my enthusiasm to dampen. By
October 21, I was writing glumly in the old weather journal:
"Today is gray; there was some rain early this morning and
then some sprinkles. Now light rain is falling, it's chilly, and
it's supposed to rain for the next four days. We'll see. Even
on days when it doesn't rain, it never feels really dry. The sun
is noticeably lower in the sky and never mops up the leftover
wetness from the last shower. Soggy and green. The light's
getting thin. Even when the sun is out it looks like there's a
scrim of milky plastic wrap over everything. And that weary
winter feel is in my bones, especially in the morning when
I wake up and feel chill, grim, gray, and dark. Autumn in
Seattle." October 23 brought a burst of afternoon showers;

the next day was an "all-day drizzler." On October 27 it was pouring down in buckets with a stiff and gusty south wind. By mid-November, my journal was starting to sound a lot like Lewis and Clark's: "Some rain today; showers fell this morning; rained off and on last night. Mid-November: That's usually when the exhilaration dies out and the despair takes over."

Because of this sudden upswing of sogginess, autumn in the Northwest lacks one of the essential defining qualities of autumn elsewhere in the country: crispness. Novelist Tom Robbins, who grew up with some semblance of crisp autumns in the hills of North Carolina before relocating to western Washington in the late 1960s, captured the essence of our autumnal crisplessness in his first novel, *Another Roadside Attraction:* "October lies on the Skagit like a wet rag on a salad. Trapped beneath low clouds, the valley is damp and green and full of sad memories. The people of the valley have far less to be unhappy about than many who live elsewhere in America, but, still, an aboriginal sadness clings like the dew to their region; their land has a blurry beauty (as if the Creator started to erase it but had second thoughts), it has dignity, fertility and hints of inner meaning—but nothing can seem to make it laugh."

It takes some getting used to, this mild damp green of autumn. Newcomers like me tend to revel in the surprises of their first rainy season—*it's not really as bad as everyone said it would be; at least there's no ice to chip off the windshield; roses in November!*—and then retrench year by year, as what Robbins poetically called the "Sung dynasty mists" hang on. Some of us, finally, throw in the towel. Others join the natives in going hatless, umbrellaless, raincoatless in all weather. Once you hear yourself say, "Yes, it's raining, but it's not really a *wet*

rain," you know you're over the hump. I was amused to see
David Blaine, Seattle's first Methodist minister, and his wife
Catharine cycle through this familiar round of meteorological
reactions in the letters they wrote to family back East in the
mid-1850s. "We had a somewhat rainy day on Sunday," David
wrote from Olympia on November 22, 1853, "but the rest of
the time since we came into the Sound has been pleasant, just
cool enough to feel well with winter clothes on. It is said it
does not freeze here at all. They plant potatoes here in February." Catharine glowed with pride in a letter to her in-laws
from their new home in Seattle the following autumn: "The
weather is very pleasant for this time of year. We have had but
little rain and no frost. We did have two or three light frosts
about a month ago but they did not kill our tomato vines and
we have plenty of ripe ones. The air, however, feels like fall
and those trees which lose their leaves show that they feel it,
but we can hardly realize it." But over the next couple of
years a note of exasperation crept in. "I never spent so
gloomy a day, I think, cold, dark, and rainy," Catharine wrote
as the 1855 rainy season got under way. By December 1, she
dismissed the weather curtly: "We have not had any real cold
weather yet, have had but a very few frosty nights, but the
weather is unpleasant, rainy and windy, making it disagreeable
for those who are obliged to be out."

Other early settlers, particularly those lured out by climatic propaganda, expressed considerably more bitterness
about the rainy realities of Oregon Territory. The Reverend
Eliah White, after a taste of autumn in 1838, wrote that the
Oregon rains were not gentle and light, as he had been led to
believe, but "extremely irksome and disagreeable . . . continuous, soaking rains." "Very rainy dull weather; warm," a pioneer of the mid-1840s complained to his journal as the rainy
season took hold in early December. "I am not certain for

health, and even for pleasure, but I should prefer a New York winter. . . . The emigrants over the mountains have a very wet introduction to this land; it must be discouraging to them. We came in the first of June, the most favorable time; perhaps our first impressions were too elevated; at any rate these dull and cloudy months with almost ceaseless rains and high sweeping ruinous waters have had some effect upon our very high estimation of this land." As the memorably named Hezekiah Packingham wrote to his brother in 1847, "Don't believe all that is said about Oregon, as many falsehoods are uttered respecting the country."

Fast-forward a century and a half and the autumn rains are still inspiring perplexed, exasperated commentary—only now we've injected a note of self-deprecating humor. "It's not the amount of rain that defines the Northwest. It's the persistence," *Seattle Times* columnist Terry McDermott wrote in a recent meditation on the rainy season. "Our rain is a relative you thought you knew until the day he showed up on your doorstep. He came in for the night, stayed through the weekend. Monday, he missed his plane. By Thursday, he had migrated from the spare room to the kitchen to the living room, devouring space as he went. Pretty soon he'd taken control of the refrigerator, the television and the stereo. Eventually, it dawns on you, he's taken over your life. Rain moves in and sets up shop in the imagination. It takes over, closing you off, obscuring. By making everything dark, it leaves no choice but to contemplate the incomprehensible." After all this time, we still can't believe our rains are for real. They're just too weird.

McDermott titled his essay "In Praise of Rain," and if he really meant it, he and his fellow rain-lovers should rejoice to learn that we may be heading into a wet spell. Not just a rainy year or two—but possibly an exceptionally rainy *decade or two.* Climatologists now speculate that weather in the Northwest, especially autumn and winter weather, runs in decadal cycles—kind of like the Biblical seven lean years and seven fat years. We've just had our lean years: for fifteen of the eighteen years between 1976 and 1994, for instance, Seattle had below-normal precipitation. And then, starting with the rainy season of 1995–96, the heavens opened with a vengeance. October, November, and December 1995 brought a total of 20.7 inches of rain to Seattle (nearly 40 percent more than normal), and the wet continued right on through January, February, March, April, and May. Western Oregon has also been getting soaked. Nehalem, on Oregon's north coast, received 37.03 inches of rain in November 1995, and Portland topped Seattle's brimming rain buckets with 11.15 inches that month. In Oregon the following November, a single rainstorm dumped 4.03 inches on Eugene and 4 inches on Corvallis, and a mud slide precipitated by the excessive rain killed four people northwest of Roseburg. By the end of 1996, Portland had broken its all-time annual rainfall record with 63.2 inches, considerably topping the previous record of 51.09 inches set in 1950 (as measured by data collected at the Portland airport). Fat years.

It may be comforting to know that some previous rainy cycles have been even wetter. According to Northwest weather historian Steve Mierzejewski, 1810–20 was the wettest decade ever known, and the period of 1841–50 was also quite wet in Oregon. The nine-year period from 1893 to 1902 was another damp phase, with over 40 inches of rain falling annually on Seattle for five of those years. Yes, 1995 was wet—42.54 inches of rain for Seattle; but 1968 was wetter—48.14 inches of rain. As it turns out, 1996 has proven to be wetter still—51.73 inches of rain fell on Sea-Tac airport, approaching the all-time record of 55.14 set in 1950. The year 1950 also brought twenty-nine consecutive days of rain to Portland. Very fat.

It seems that we're doomed (or blessed) with a climate of extremes—very wet rainy seasons alternating with unusually dry ones. Here in the Northwest, come autumn, the abnormal is normal.

Rain is not the only weather story that hits in autumn. Wind speeds also pick up after the tranquil summer months, and every few years a major windstorm slams the Pacific Northwest. The biggest of all, at least since records have been kept, was the Columbus Day blow of 1962. The storm began east of the Philippines as a typhoon (the Pacific brand of hurricane) named Freda, and in the first week of October it migrated across the ocean, picked up energy, expanded and intensified, and finally bore down mightily on the Northwest coast. The typhoon generated three distinct "waves" that broke on the Oregon coast between October 11 and 13—but the climax came on October 12, when winds reached 131 miles per hour at Oregon's Mount Hebo Air Force station, 116 miles per hour in Portland, and 160 miles per hour at the Naselle radar site in Washington's Pacific County. High winds on the coast lasted for three to five hours, and when the storm moved inland it concentrated its fury on the heavily populated region west of the Cascades. A corridor of 1,000 miles from northern California to British Columbia got smashed by this storm. The toll in Washington and Oregon was horrific: 46 people dead and another 317 requiring hospitalization, 15 billion board feet of timber blown down (some of which was salvaged), 53,000 homes damaged. The winds overturned cars, knocked down church spires and statues, buckled bridges, ripped part of the roof off Portland's

Multnomah Stadium, and brought down the twin 520-foot
steel towers that carried the main power lines to Portland. At
the height of the storm, 500,000 houses were without power.
Total damage was estimated at $170 million in Oregon and
$50 million in Washington.

Forecasters, checking the record books, reassured people
that the Northwest was unlikely to get hit by a second windstorm of this severity for at least another twenty-five years.
As it turns out, they were off by seven years. The windstorm
of December 12, 1995, though not quite of the magnitude of
the 1962 Columbus Day blow, was a whopper. Winds reached
119 miles per hour at Sea Lion Caves on the Oregon coast,
and the courthouse of the coastal town of Newport clocked
one gust at 107 miles per hour. In one particular, the December
1995 windstorm topped the Columbus Day blow: at Astoria
in northwest Oregon, barometric pressure fell to the lowest
level ever recorded in the state (see Chapter Four for more
details). Seattle was spared the worst of the storm, but things
still got pretty wild here. Foolishly, I was out driving as the
winds began to really pick up. There was so much damp debris
on the roads that it was like driving through green slush. When
I tried to turn around and go home, I found the road blocked
by a tree that had fallen, taking a power line with it. Five minutes earlier and it would have fallen on me. When I finally did
get home, by a different route, power was out on both sides
of the Sound. It was incredibly eerie to look out the window
to perfect blackness. It wasn't the worst storm in history, but
it was a sobering reminder of the power the atmosphere can
unleash when it's in the mood. There are teeth behind the mild
smile of the Northwest.

Seattle founding father Arthur Denny mentioned an autumn
windstorm in his memoir *Pioneer Days on Puget Sound:* "The
heaviest wind storm since the settlement of the country was

on the night of November 16, 1875. This was simply a strong
gale which threw down considerable timber and overturned
light structures, such as sheds and out buildings." Western
Washington and Oregon also took a hit from a major windstorm on October 21, 1934. Winds of seventy miles an
hour scoured Seattle, blowing off roofs, overturning fishing
boats, and lifting a hangar at Boeing Field off the ground
and dropping it on top of four planes. On the waterfront,
the trans-Pacific liner *President Madison* came unmoored and
rammed into a steamboat, sinking it. Eighteen people died in
that storm. Ceaseless drizzle looks positively benign next to
weather events like these.

"So what if they paid in wetness for the mild climate," mused
the hero of Bernard Malamud's novel *A New Life* during his
first rainy season in western Oregon, "the warmth made up
for rain." Wet and mild are the fungusy twins of our Northwest autumns. But every now and then an arctic blast in
autumn sends the twins running for their lives. The most
severe fall freeze in recorded history hit in November 1955.
Strong north winds carried arctic air into Washington on the
morning of November 11, with temperatures ranging from
10° to 15° west of the Cascades and from 0° to 10° east of
the mountains. Temperatures kept on falling until November
15, when they bottomed out at 0° to 15° on the west side and
0° to −19° on the east side. The temperature at Sea-Tac airport fell to 6° on November 15, and even Astoria on the coast
recorded a low of 15°. The freeze was especially damaging
because it hit so early in the season, before plants and trees
had gone dormant. Harvests of apples, root crops, and late-
season vegetables were spoiled. Fruit trees and berry vines
suffered extensive damage, and tender ornamentals died
throughout the Northwest. The Washington Park Arboretum

in Seattle reported well over 1,000 rhododendrons and 350 camellias lost to the freeze. It was indeed a black week for the region's gardeners.

November has also on occasion brought significant snow-fall to western Washington and Oregon. On November 18, 1946, 9.4 inches of snow fell on Seattle, and November 1985 brought a total of 17.5 inches, with heavy snows falling on November 21 and 27. Global warming has not yet prevented such events; 1996 saw yet another wintry outbreak, with 7 inches of snow blanketing metropolitan Seattle on November 19. The storm even made the national news, and relatives and friends of mine from the East Coast and California called to commiserate. Congratulations would have been more in order as far as I was concerned: for the few days the snow stayed on the ground, the city never looked lovelier.

Chapter Four

*"Remarkably
equable"*

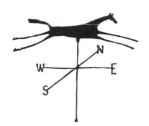

SCIENTISTS'
WEATHER

FTER A DEEP IMMERSION IN THE
outbursts of overwrought pioneers
and early settlers, what a relief it is
to approach the cool, stately temple of science. Here is a sanctu-
ary of pure objectivity, where facts are everything and feelings are
nothing. Data, formula, analysis, forecast, verification: this, in
theory, in a nutshell, is what the science of weather is all about.

In theory. In reality, the weather of the Pacific Northwest has
always had a way of overwhelming and warping objectivity. The
weather out here is so intense, so peculiar, so encrusted with
mythology and notoriety that meteorologists sometimes become
as impassioned as poets. This was especially true in the early days
of weather science back in the late nineteenth century. Papers
that opened with sober climatic analysis devolved into spirited
defenses and outright boosterism. *It's not as bad as people think* was

the loud subtext of pioneering Northwest meteorological inves-
tigations. There were celebrations of the mildness of the temperatures and the gentleness of the rains, and extravagant claims that
the Northwest maritime climate promoted good health, long life,
high productivity, and an all-over glow of intellectual and physical
well-being. Even today, in the era of Doppler radar and high-resolution computer models, Northwest weather scientists tend to
be an enthusiastic, excitable lot. "I'm here because I fell in love
with local weather," confesses Cliff Mass, who was raised in New
York State and is now a professor of atmospheric sciences at the
University of Washington. "We're not all clinical, cold-blooded
Mr. Spock types. We love intense weather. When the weather
gets interesting, people go crazy." Craziness seems to be paying
off, for weather science in the Northwest has really hit its stride
in the past couple of years.

Our region has always been a favorite with weather scientists,
perhaps because our climate is so different from what they
expected it to be. From the time of Aristotle and Parmenides of
Ela until well into the mid-nineteenth century, students of meteorology took it for granted that latitude was the prime factor in
determining a region's climate. In fact, the English word "climate"
derives from the Greek *klima,* meaning inclination—which in
meteorology refers to the inclination or angle of the sun above
the horizon. Judging from the inclination of the sun, Seattle
should have the same climate as Quebec, Newfoundland, and
central Mongolia. Why doesn't it? Why is it so much more temperate here—warmer in winter, cooler in summer? This was the
first question weather scientists in the region set out to answer.

One of the earliest, and most eloquent, treatments of the subject appeared in 1872 in a booklet entitled "Climates of the Northwest" written by the Honorable Selecius Garfielde, a "delegate in Congress from Washington Territory," as the title page proudly declared. In his paper, Garfielde acknowledged the notion that climate was determined by latitude: after a spin of the globe, he wrote, "the inference is at once drawn that [Puget Sound] possesses a bleak and inhospitable climate." But "this conclusion," he hastened to say, "is very far from the truth." In fact, to his mind, Puget Sound had the winters of Norfolk, Virginia, and the summers of Nova Scotia. The explanation was a simple one: the region's proximity to the Pacific Ocean, "the largest area on the surface of the globe which presents an even spherical surface." In the winter months, southwesterly winds "sweep forward with almost uninterrupted regularity" over the ocean water, which moderates the air temperature. The warming is further enhanced in winter, according to Garfielde, by the influence of ocean currents. Taken together, the prevailing onshore winds and the ocean currents "fully account for the mildness of the winters" from San Francisco north to Sitka.

Garfielde was on pretty solid ground as far as the impact of the ocean and southwest winds are concerned, but his argument got a little shaky when he brought in the ocean currents. A good chunk of his booklet was devoted to the workings of the mysterious Japanese current—a river in the Pacific, as Garfielde explained it, that rose in the Indian Ocean, moved north along the east shore of Asia, hit the Aleutian Islands, and split in two, whereupon one branch passed east through the Arctic Ocean while the other branch bent south along North America's West

Coast until it dissipated at Cape Mendocino. It is this second branch that supposedly had such a pronounced influence on our weather. Since the current's temperature hardly fluctuated at all with the seasons, averaging 50° in winter and 52° in summer, it acted as a natural temperature regulator for the maritime regions, especially Puget Sound. As Garfielde wrote, "No other portion of the Pacific Coast is influenced to the same extent in its climatic conditions by the Japan Current as the districts bordering on the waters of Puget Sound." The reason for this, he wrote, was the daily ebb and flow of tides: 50 thousand million cubic yards of water poured in and out of the Sound each day, and every tide brought in "a fresh supply of water of uniform temperature" from the Japanese current. Garfielde summed up: "Puget Sound acts as an immense *heater* to moderate the rigors of winter, and as a *refrigerator* to cool the air during the heated term." It was one of America's great natural wonders, as regular and inspiring as Old Faithful.

It may come as a surprise to some that Garfielde's claims about the Japanese current are *totally unfounded,* for the notion has proved to be astonishingly tenacious. Journalist Walter Rue, in his 1978 book *Weather of the Pacific Coast,* wrote of the uncanny "persistence of the myth about the current," which in his day was still taught in schools and trotted out as established fact on television quiz shows. Even today I've heard amateur weather buffs assert in full confidence that the current accounts for our mild winters. This is all the more surprising since the theory was debunked at least as far back as 1899. In a paper entitled "The Mild Temperature of the Pacific Northwest and the Influence of the 'Kuro Siwo,'" Beamer S. Pague, the founder of the Oregon State

Weather Bureau and one of the pioneers of Northwest climatological research, stated conclusively that the atmospheric influence of the current is negligible: it is too narrow to have much impact on the temperature of the air flowing over it, and in any case, during the winter months its average temperature is only two degrees warmer than that of the surrounding ocean waters. The current theory, in a word, is hogwash. Nonetheless, nearly eighty years after Pague's paper, Walter Rue still felt obliged to "explode" the "myth" of the current in capital letters: "The current does NOT appreciably influence Seattle's weather. It is NOT responsible for mild winters in Western Washington, Western Oregon, and parts of British Columbia." I'll say it again: Kuro Siwo current, begone!

I hate to knock the Honorable Selecius Garfielde too hard, for aside from the Japanese current business, his little treatise is charming and, in its own way, fairly accurate. The weather of the Northwest clearly inspired him, and he was only too happy to move from analyzing local conditions to singing their praises. He trilled over the southwest winds of winter that give the landscape "a carpet of perpetual verdure" and the northwest winds of summer that make the atmosphere "fresh and exhilarating" with nights that are "clear and deliciously cool; thus enabling nature to restore the energies exhausted during the day." Seattle, he noted with a touch of civic pride, has the same mean temperature as "Pekin," London, New York, and Chicago: this was no coincidence but rather a direct result of "man's intuitive perceptions in determining the belt of the earth's surface best adapted to his physical and intellectual development by promoting health and longevity and stimulating the highest activities." By virtue of its superior climate, Garfielde claimed, Seattle would in time be "worthy of its place as a link in the capital chain which encircles the world."

This was rather a bold assertion back in 1872, when the future world "capital" was not much more than a boomtown hacked out of the firs and cedars—but similar claims crop up repeatedly in our weather history. Frances Fuller Victor, an early Northwest travel writer, insisted in her 1872 volume *All Over Oregon and Washington* that the country east of the Cascades was uniquely health-enhancing: "Without marshes or any local causes of miasma, with a clear, dry atmosphere, warmed by sun, and cooled by the vicinity of snow mountains, [this region] could never be unhealthy." Pioneer Ezra Meeker devoted an entire chapter of his *Seventy Years of Progress in Washington* (1921) to health and longevity. Beginning with the rather remarkable statistic that the death rate in Washington state for 1915–17 was nearly half the national average (13.7 deaths per 1,000 in twenty-six reporting states, compared with only 7.8 deaths per 1,000 in Washington), Meeker undertook to explain it as a consequence of our superior climate: "The equable climate of Washington lays a solid foundation for good health and longevity. The absence of extreme heat or cold . . . abundantly proves this fact. Then it is scientifically proven that a moist atmosphere is a clean atmosphere. That when rain falls, or fog prevails, the air, so to speak, is washed and all impurity, if any, is removed, of which there is precious little coming from the wide sweep of the Pacific Ocean and carried inland far beyond the eastern confines of the State by the prevailing winds." Though Meeker's syntax got a little shaky by the end, his point is clear—and he recapped it, and indeed stretched it out a bit, at the chapter's end: "With the pure air, pure water, and most equable climate, Washington heads the list as the most healthy spot on earth. I do not write this in a vainglorious, optimistic mood, but as a record of a sincere belief, resulting from painstaking research for facts to prepare for writing this chapter. It has been a revelation." (Meeker would be interested to learn that as of 1994, Washington's death rate was still lower than the national average—747.9 per 100,000 residents compared with a national rate of 875.4; but a number of states had rates that were lower still, and the lowest of all was Utah's at 548.9: so much for Washington's claim to be the "most healthy spot on earth.")

This line of thought received its ultimate expression in a strange little pamphlet published in 1924 under the grandiloquent title *In the Zone of Filtered Sunshine: Why the Pacific Northwest Is Destined to Dominate the Commercial World*. This was the work of one Erwin L. Weber, billed on the title page as a member of the American Society of Mechanical Engineers and the American Society of Heating and Ventilating Engineers. Weber was also something of a visionary; he saw literal clouds of glory streaming over the Northwest skies. "Filtered sunshine" was his euphemism for good old Northwest gloom, and to his way of thinking, gloom was great, gloom was healthy, gloom was the very fountain of life: "Humidity and clouds are nature's great blanket, which intercepts the radiation of heat to and from the earth, and equalizes its temperature. Without them the earth would each day become a huge frying pan, and at night a huge refrigerator. Without them life upon this planet would become extinct."

Not only did clouds make the earth habitable, they provided the environment in which people grew best and learned most—

the cloudier the skies, the more people flourished. In a section headed "The False Gospel of Sunshine," Weber insisted that "progressive and energetic men and women were not developed basking in the sunshine on a pile of sand, or seated under the shade of a palm tree," but rather working briskly and efficiently in regions with "less than 2000 hours of intense sunshine per annum." By this reckoning, the Pacific Northwest was a veritable hotbed of human superiority—"one of those few favored regions which possesses all the basic requirements necessary and desirable for the development of the most virile types of humanity . . . the most energetic peoples . . . and the highest attainments of civilization."

The trouble, for contemporary readers, is that Weber's definition of the "most energetic peoples" is pretty much identical to Hitler's—"Nordic Europe, embracing the British Isles, Northern France and Germany, Holland, Denmark, Belgium and Southern Scandinavia." Weber explained, with dubious reasoning, that when residents of these cloudy lands emigrated to the eastern seaboard of the United States, they floundered because they were not adapted to the climate: "The summers were too hot and oppressive, the winters were too cold, and the glare of sunshine was too great." But here in the Pacific Northwest, the Nordic races felt right at home, for this was "the only part of the North American continent with a climate and environment identical with that of the homeland—the cradle of the race." Leave New York, Chicago, and Philadelphia to the "Balkan, Polish, Slavic and Semitic types." Leave southern California to "the Mediterranean races," who can handle "the intensity of sunshine." But save the cloudy Northwest for the "progressive and energetic men and women" of the Nordic races. Already, Weber observed, the people who lived here "moved about and worked faster, more deliberately and steadier than in other localities," and they produced healthier offspring. These promising signs were but heralds of a triumphant Aryan future. Weber concluded with a trumpet volley of lofty claims: "Vast natural resources of timber and minerals. Copious quantities of pure glacial water and unlimited hydro electric power. . . . The healthiest climate in the world. With these God-given advantages there can be no question of the ultimate destiny of the Pacific Northwest; to dominate the commercial world. How soon this will evolve depends solely upon how rapidly the manifold advantages of the Pacific Northwest are made known to those in whom the 'homing instinct' is still left unsatisfied."

Strip away the racism and one is left with a rather bizarre fusion of pseudoscience and civic boosterism. After reading through Weber's extravagant claims about the region's imminent dominion over the commercial world, I was not surprised to discover that *In the Zone of Filtered Sunshine* was distributed by the Seattle Chamber of Commerce. Dreams of glory and riches have risen on even feebler foundations.

More serious, and more recognizably rational, weather science began in our region in the late nineteenth century with the work of the aforementioned Beamer S. Pague. A native of Pennsylvania, Pague had cut his meteorological teeth as a weather observer for the U.S. Signal Service (the earliest precursor of the National Weather Service) on New Hampshire's notoriously inclement Mount Washington. Here he was exposed, according to a biographical sketch in H. K. Hines's *An Illustrated History of the State of Oregon* (1893), to "great hardships and much severe weather" for fifteen months. Perhaps as a result, Pague decided to migrate west, to San Francisco in 1885 and on to Oregon the next year. He lived in Roseburg for a couple of years and then moved to Portland, where he took charge of the weather station in 1888. The following year Pague helped push through the establishment of the Oregon State Weather Service and then served as its director, working with the Signal Service on the collection of accurate meteorological data and the issuing of timely forecasts and storm warnings. Pague was a man with a mission: he was determined to set the record straight on Northwest weather, "to prove," as one historian wrote, "that impressions could be false, that western Oregon was not really as rainy as it seemed." Pague's 1893 volume, *Second Biennial Report of the Oregon Weather Bureau Cooperating with the United States Department of Agriculture,* marshaled an impressive array of statistics demonstrating that Portland really has about the same annual rainfall as New York and Philadelphia, and considerably less than New Orleans. As far as temperature was concerned, Portland stacked up as a pleasant, moderate alternative to cold Chicago and hot New Orleans. The sole justification Pague found for Oregon's "webfoot" image was the average number of rainy days per year: 156 compared to 128 in New York and 127 in Washington, D.C. Rain, he concluded, far from being a curse, was one of the region's most precious resources, for "due to the fulsome supply of moisture during the year," crop failures never afflicted the fertile Willamette Valley.

While Pague dedicated himself to documenting the climatological norms for the state of Oregon, the Signal Service embarked on its own comprehensive weather study of the entire Northwest region. The findings appeared in an 1888 report prepared under the direction of Adolphus Washington Greely, then serving as the army's chief signal officer. Greely's name on the title page guaranteed the document serious consideration, for the man had become something of a national hero after leading the first official American expedition to the Arctic. Greely's party headed into the frozen north in 1881 with the goal of setting up thirteen circumpolar meteorological stations, but tragedy overtook them. During the winter of 1883, after relief parties had twice failed to intercept the expedition, seventeen of Greely's men froze or starved to death. It wasn't until the spring of 1884 that U.S. Navy Commander Winfield Scott Schley succeeded in rescuing Greely and the six surviving members of his team. Greely subsequently rose swiftly through the ranks of the Signal Service, and in 1887 he became the first volunteer and enlisted man to attain the rank of chief signal officer and brigadier general.

Greely's report on the climate of Oregon and Washington Territory, transmitted by the Secretary of War to the U.S. Senate on October 20, 1888, makes for interesting reading—as interesting for its *denials* as for its *assertions*. Plainly the prime motive of the study was to deflate the most pernicious Northwest climatic myths, particularly the myth of superabundant, ceaseless rainfall. Greely made his case clear in the first few pages: "Although the rain-fall along the immediate coast of the Pacific Ocean, ranging from 70 to over 107 inches, is the heaviest in the United States, yet, contrary to the generally-received opinion, this enormous rain-fall does not cover the entire area of these States, but only 6 per centum of them." The generally received opinion that "the rain is continuous . . . during the wet season" is also false, he argued. In fact, Signal Service statistics proved that even on the coast "every other day in October and March is without rain, while in intervening months the frequency of rain is somewhat greater, rising in December to three days out of four"; away from the coast, the incidence of rainfall drops to every other day, even at the height of the rainy season. Greely was equally adamant in correcting the "fallacy" that eastern Oregon and Washington are "almost rainless." In fact, "the area over which less than 10 inches of rain falls does not cover 5 per centum of either state."

So—6 percent too wet and 5 percent too dry leaves 89 percent pretty much just right. Just right especially for farming, which was still the dominant enterprise in the region. Greely waxed lyrical about the joys and profits of Pacific Northwest agriculture: "Nearly all of Oregon and Washington Territory experiences very dry Julys and Augusts; the rain-fall, fortunately for these States, being deficient, while clear and sunshiny days are particularly frequent at that season of the year when the staple crops have fully ripened. The alternation of wet and dry seasons renders it possible for crops to be raised, with certainty that the rain-fall will come during certain months, and be followed later by fair weather suitable for harvesting."

Moderate, "remarkably equable temperature conditions" are another climatic blessing of the region, Greely wrote, noting with approval that the winter mean temperature of over half the area is above freezing and that prolonged spells of freezing weather afflict only the higher elevations of the Columbian plains and the high plateaus of southeastern Oregon. Summers "in the neighborhood of Puget Sound and along the coast" are similarly mild and "remarkably . . . comfortable." "Variability," which Greely defined as the change in daily mean temperature from one day to the next, is rarely more than one degree in Washington and Oregon and is often less, "thus showing in these States an equability of temperature which is unequaled in any other part of the United States, except along the immediate coast line in California, from Cape Mendocino to San Diego."

Putting temperature and rainfall statistics together, Greely wrapped up the introduction to the report with a glowing portrait of a meteorological Eden: "To summarize, Oregon and Washington are favored with a climate of unusual mildness and equability; while the immediate coast regions have very heavy rain falls, yet such rain occurs during the winter months of December to February, and in all cases the wet season gives place gradually to the dry season, during July and August. While the preponderating amount of rain falls during the winter, yet the spring, early summer, and late fall are all marked by moderate rains at not infrequent intervals."

This is climatology just a whisker shy of propaganda—propaganda aimed at new settlers—and Greely even went so far as to assure prospective farmers that "most cereals and other important staple crops" would thrive "to a marked extent" in the Northwest. No mention was made of the frigid cow-killer winters that gripped the region in the 1840s, 1850s, and early 1860s, the floods that periodically inundate prime Willamette farmland when warm rains melt heavy mountain snowpacks, or the occasional droughts that shrivel crops and turn forests into tinder for raging fires. Greely might have replied that he was interested in establishing norms and averages, not documenting extreme acts of God. But there is no denying that this is science with a subtext. Greely had a message and a motive, and they come through loud and clear. As historian Richard Maxwell Brown wrote in "Rainfall and History: Perspectives on the Pacific Northwest," "Greely's report . . . proved to be the core document in the scientific campaign to validate the high quality of the Pacific Northwest climate and to diminish the reputation of excessive rain. . . . The curse of excessive rainfall was denied, and, as of 1888, the farmers of the Great Plains, whose own climate was now entering one of its most severe dry periods in history, had government assurance that optimum weather conditions awaited those who emigrated to the Pacific Northwest, as indeed thousands were to do."

But despite Greely's best efforts, the "curse of excessive rainfall" has persisted in the public imagination, and weather scientists keep whacking away at it with ever more elaborate and authoritative arrays of statistics. One of the more stinging modern-day whacks was delivered by Phil Church in the December 1974 issue of *Weatherwise*. Church, who had recently retired from his chairmanship of the University of Washington department of atmospheric sciences, exhaustively and ingeniously analyzed some seventy-five years of climatological records in a paper entitled "Some Precipitation Characteristics of Seattle." Right off the bat, Church established the fact that Seattle's rainy reputation is totally unjustified: from 1893 to 1970, Seattle's median yearly rainfall was just 33.83 inches, which is about the same as that of Dallas, Kansas City, Chicago, Cleveland, and Burlington, Vermont, and about half that of Miami and New Orleans. But yearly totals are just the tip of the iceberg. Church delved deeper into the climatological minutiae in order to calibrate how many rainy *hours* we get each year, and he arrived at a rather startling conclusion: "While many visitors and a few others temporarily stationed in Seattle complain that it rains all the time, simple arithmetic shows that it rains (mean annual) a mere 11% of the time"—22 percent in January, but under 3 percent in July. But the coup de grace was his classification of rainfall intensities from "light drizzle" (.01 inch or less per hour) through drizzle, light rain, and so on, all the way up to heavy rain (.16 inch or more per hour). By Church's reckoning, 72.5 percent of Seattle's precipitation takes the form of drizzle, 19.8 percent is light rain, 6.2 percent moderate rain, and only 1.5 percent heavy rain. And so, he summed up with a gleeful flourish, "Because of the preponderance of 'drizzle' intensities one might truthfully say that it rarely 'rains' in Seattle." It's hard to understand how "the curse of excessive rainfall" could ever recover from this death blow—but such is the phoenixlike power of a bad meteorological reputation.

There is "no science susceptible of more development, nor is there a science which will yield more valuable results than the science of meteorology," Beamer Pague declared in 1899. Pague knew better than anyone how far meteorology had come in the Northwest and how far it still had to go before "valuable results" showed up. He and Greely had done a creditable job of documenting Northwest climate norms, laying the foundation for local meteorology. But forecasters still had only a dim understanding of the region's atmospheric peculiarities and an even dimmer sense of how to translate this understanding into weather forecasts. The state of the art was still fairly primitive.

At the end of the nineteenth century, the telegraph was probably the most valuable meteorological tool. Since weather systems generally move from west to east in this country, a forecaster could get a good idea of what was coming by looking at conditions at telegraph offices to the west. Telegraphic communication was the basis of America's first national weather network, organized by the fledgling Smithsonian Institution back in 1849. The Smithsonian distributed standardized weather instruments to local telegraph offices around the country, and in exchange the offices agreed to clear their lines each morning by transmitting weather observations to Washington, D.C. The readings, collected and analyzed at the Smithsonian, were used to create a daily weather map that was mounted in the great hall of the Smithsonian "castle." In time, Northwest telegraph offices at Olympia, Spokane, Portland, and Roseburg became part of this meteorological network, which was turned over to the federal government when Congress established a national weather service in 1870. Unfortunately, the national telegraphic network did not really benefit forecasters on the West Coast since it failed to incorporate readings from the eastern Pacific, where our weather comes from. With no telegraph offices out in the ocean and no weather observers there aside from mariners, data were sparse. This information gap continues to plague meteorologists in the Northwest and is one reason why forecasting can be trickier here than in some other parts of the country.

Meteorology made but slow and fitful progress in the first decades of this century. The invention of the airplane gave forecasters an eye on the upper atmosphere, and communication of weather observations became faster and easier with the proliferation of telephones, radio, and teletype. But for the most part, these were refinements, not breakthroughs. Weather science remained pretty much the same ball game until the second half of the twentieth century, when three critical inventions changed the rules: radar, which was perfected during World War II and used by Weather Bureau meteorologists starting in 1946; the high-speed electronic computer, first used to create numerical forecast models in the 1940s; and the satellite, which has been providing images of the earth's atmosphere since April 1, 1960, when TIROS I (Television Infrared Observation Satellite) began orbiting the poles at about 500 miles out in space.

Radar, computer-generated models, and satellite imagery have been part of the forecasting repertoire for nearly half a century, but here in the Northwest, meteorologists are only now beginning to realize the full potential of these technologies. As atmospheric scientist Cliff Mass puts it, "We've learned more about local weather conditions in the last ten years than in the previous hundred years." One reason weather science is booming in the Northwest now is that numerical forecast models are finally sophisticated enough to handle local terrain. Basically, a numerical model is a computer-generated simulation of what the atmosphere is going to look like in the near future. One of the most powerful computers in the world, the Cray YMP-832 run by the National Centers for Environmental Prediction (NCEP) outside Washington, D.C., creates these models by digesting thousands of weather readings from around the world. Once the Cray "knows" what the temperature, air pressure, and humidity are at a particular moment, it uses mathematical equations based on the laws of physics to calculate how those conditions will change every twelve hours over the course of the next five days. In creating models, meteorologists impose a three-dimensional grid on the atmosphere and feed the computer readings for every grid point. Obviously, the finer the grid, the closer it approximates what one forecaster calls the "continuous fluid" of the actual atmosphere. But the problem is that the finer the grid, the more calculations the computer must carry out. More calculations mean more time—and time is of the essence in forecasting. If the computer can't produce the model before the forecaster needs to send out the forecast, it's worthless.

Back in the early days of modeling, when computers were slower and far less powerful than they are today, grid points were spaced 381 kilometers apart. That meant that the complex, bumpy, water-invaded terrain of the Pacific Northwest was essentially erased: on a grid of 381 kilometers, the region looked pretty much like Kansas. But you don't have to be a meteorologist to know that weather systems behave very differently here than they do in Kansas. Mountains and water do funny things to our weather, funneling wind currents through gaps and gorges, squeezing moisture out of clouds in odd ways, blocking the smooth progression of fronts, forcing air to take a kind of roller-coaster ride as it moves inland. After a couple of seasons, any forecaster worth his or her salt develops an intuitive "gut" sense of how regional topography affects the weather—but now weather scientists are making intuition obsolete with more refined models and other new technologies that take into account the complexities of our terrain. In a sense, Pacific Northwest weather is finally on the map.

Northwest weather science is also on the map in a whole new way. Mass, who is at the forefront of modeling the atmosphere out here, explains what's going on:

> Right now we're in a significant period of transition—really, a paradigm shift. Our whole understanding of Pacific Northwest weather has been enhanced in the last several years. Since topography dominates the weather out here, understanding the effects of terrain is the name of the game in local forecasting. Things are opening up because we're now getting a three-dimensional view of regional circulation that we never had before. For the first time we're using computer models to simulate local effects. Right now we're running a regional model with a twelve-kilometer resolution here in the department, which means we're leading NCEP [which currently runs a daily suite of models at resolutions of between twenty-nine and eighty kilometers]. And once high-resolution, real-time computer models come online, it will bring *real* change to the forecasting process.

Mass is also enthusiastic about the new weather instruments, including Doppler radar (known in the business as 88D) and a wind profiler (a specialized radar used to measure wind speed and direction), that have been installed as part of the ongoing National Weather Service modernization process. Says Mass:

> With the 88D radar on Camano Island and the profiler at the National Weather Service forecast office at Sand Point [on Lake Washington, northeast of downtown

Seattle], we're getting a view we never had before. The 88D is showing detailed structures that we didn't know about before. We're seeing rain shadows in a way we never imagined. The new satellites are mapping out wind and precipitation fields. We've never had anything like this.

One highly visible payoff of the new weather technology is in forecasting a local meteorological phenomenon known as the Puget Sound convergence zone. As Brad Colman, the science and operations officer at the Seattle National Weather Service forecast office, explains, the Puget Sound convergence zone results from the interaction of surface winds with the topography of northwestern Washington. There are two major openings on either side of the Olympic Mountains: to the north, the Strait of Juan de Fuca; to the south, the Chehalis Gap. These openings lead into a basin formed by the solid wall of the Cascade Range to the east. A convergence zone occurs when moisture-laden westerly winds blow through both openings and are forced by the Cascades to meet in the Puget Sound basin, producing what Colman terms a "significantly enhanced band of precipitation"—or, in other words, a localized downpour. The interesting thing about a convergence zone is that skies can be clear to the north and south while, in the zone itself, rain comes down in buckets. Typically, a convergence zone occurs after a front has passed through: if you're watching the sky, you'll note that the rain that blew in on the south wind has stopped, but just when you expect the clouds to clear off, a north wind kicks up, bringing down a band of showers—sometimes heavy and persistent ones. Convergence zones generally form north of Seattle—from about Everett down to the King–Snohomish County line—and they're most common in spring and early summer. On average, a Puget Sound convergence zone forms about twenty to thirty times each year. Enough rainfall accumulates from springtime convergence zones that precipitation levels generally hold steady in Everett between April and June while declining noticeably at Olympia and Boeing Field.

Cliff Mass notes that as recently as the 1950s, atmospheric scientists did not understand that convergence zones are "orographically induced" (created by the mountains): "Back then, they really didn't know much about them. They called a convergence zone a 'secondary cold front.'" Mass became fascinated by the phenomenon while he was in graduate school in the 1970s, and in 1981 he published the seminal paper on the subject. But since then, we've learned a good deal more about how, when, and where convergence zones form, thanks in large part to Mass's high-resolution forecast model and the installation of Doppler radar in February 1994. Today Mass makes the formula for a convergence zone sound like an atmospheric cake recipe: "It all depends on wind direction on the coast and how stable the air is. When there is a west and northwest flow with stable air, you get a convergence zone on Puget Sound. The atmosphere must be relatively stable so that the air will flow around the Olympics rather than move over them."

Brad Colman, who works in close partnership with Mass on analyzing and predicting convergence zones, has a slightly different perspective. He agrees that the new technology has greatly improved our ability to observe the "three-dimensional" flow of weather across western Washington and Canada. But when it comes to the actual forecast, he is not quite as optimistic as Mass.

"Simulating a convergence zone is now a piece of cake to academics," says Colman:

> They put the data in the model, the model shows a
> convergence zone for tomorrow, and they break out
> the champagne—problem solved. But the forecaster
> who needs to describe the situation to the public has
> a different set of challenges. The models are beautiful
> and seductive, and they produce realistic bands of
> showers where showers commonly occur. But how
> accurate is their location? What the forecaster needs
> to know is that it's going to rain hard at Paine Field
> at 10 A.M. and move down to Boeing Field by 1 P.M.,
> and the models don't tell us that. So it becomes a
> question of how we are going to word the forecast.
> We're definitely going through rapid changes in our
> tools and in our understanding of Northwest weather,
> but understanding the weather and forecasting it are
> different problems. Our understanding is excellent,
> but our forecasting ability will lag slightly behind. The
> sense of celebration is premature.

The Puget Sound convergence zone is not the only meteorological peculiarity of the Pacific Northwest. Portland has its own local specialty—the wind effects of the Columbia Gorge—and this too has inspired some exciting research in recent years. Stephen K. Todd, the meteorologist in charge of the Portland National Weather Service forecast office, describes what the Gorge does to the city's weather:

> The Gorge is the only place between Canada and central California where air can flow in and out through
> a significant gap in the Cascade-Sierra mountain range.

The predominant effect is in winter. When high pressure builds up east of the mountains with cold air in place, a strong east wind will set up, bringing a blast of arctic air into the Portland region. The Gorge effect helps produce our notorious winter ice storms. When the cold east wind blowing through the Gorge meets with moist Pacific air, rain freezes on any surface. The area affected is actually rather narrow: Portland gets hit, but south Portland and Oregon City are out of it, and to the north Vancouver is out of it. The winds out of the Gorge can make Portland 10 or 15 degrees colder than the surrounding areas. The Gorge effect is frequent but not constant—we'll get it maybe ten to twenty days a year. In summer, the winds reverse and blow through the Gorge from the west.

Jack Capell, a distinguished meteorologist who has been doing the weather reports on Portland's KGW television station since 1958, says that the Columbia Gorge creates considerably more radical weather changes than the Puget Sound convergence zone: "Due to the Gorge effect, the local air mass can change rapidly from maritime to continental. If we could block up the Gorge, it would make local forecasting a lot easier." But even without the Gorge, the mountains and valleys of western Oregon can create headaches for local forecasters. Capell notes that it's often hard to tell when the Cascades will seal off the continental air of eastern Oregon from the maritime air of western Oregon and when the air masses will breach the barrier. He also emphasizes how important it is to factor in the effect of landforms on wind speeds: "Winds will be stronger when they're lined up with the valleys than when they blow against the valleys. You really try to watch this when a storm blows up from the southwest. The 1962 Columbus Day storm was a classic example of winds blowing along the valleys, which resulted in much stronger winds. It was the ideal setup for a big blow."

Capell gets credit for identifying yet another local weather oddity known as the Brookings effect—an extremely localized summertime condition in which temperatures in the immediate vicinity of Brookings on the Oregon coast rise into the 80s and 90s while the rest of the coast remains in the 60s. He explains how it works: "Brookings would report that their sea-level air pressure had dropped very low, and it was always thought to be a mistake. Now we know that a heat low moves out over Brookings due to the conformation of the land. The low forces air to sweep down the Coast Range and out to sea. It's warm to begin with and it gets even warmer as it drops downslope."

Capell says that western Oregon meteorologists have been aware of the effects of the Gorge for years, but according to Steve Todd, Portland's National Weather Service forecasters have made dramatic improvements in pinpointing the Gorge effect and other local conditions in recent years due to the new technologies: "With the 88D and the new computer models, we're beginning to see things in a new way. It used to be that we had to wait for reports from the weather balloon releases at 4 A.M. and 4 P.M. in order to monitor the winds aloft, but now we can use the 88D to see how wind patterns change and evolve. This is a huge help in forecasting the windstorm events we get here. It helps us look inside the storms and see rotation."

Todd says all the new pieces really came together in forecasting the windstorm of December 12, 1995—the most intense and most damaging autumn windstorm to hit the Northwest since the notorious Columbus Day storm of 1962: "We had the forecast two days ahead and we issued warnings twenty-four hours ahead of time. The newspapers printed the storm warnings the morning of the event—it was totally unprecedented." Dave Willson, one of the lead forecasters at the Portland office, was on top of this windstorm from the start, and he and colleague Ira Kosovitz later won an Exceptional Specific Prediction award from the American Meteorological Society for their forecasting work. Willson replays the sequence of events for me. As the storm approached, he and his colleagues at the forecast office began scrutinizing the 1962 Columbus Day windstorm for clues about how storms of that magnitude develop. They noticed that a strong wind blew ahead of the storm in 1962 and that the same thing was happening again—on Sunday, December 10, reports came in of seventy-mile-an-hour winds on the south Oregon coast out at Cape Blanco. "This was the first storm," says Willson, "and it tipped us off that another one might be following it." All signs indicated that it was shaping up to be a "classical bomb"—a rapidly developing low pressure center. Checking back through historical records, Willson was able to calculate when the bomb was likely to hit, and how hard: "Once the pressure dropped to a certain level on the coast, we knew about how many hours would elapse before winds in excess of fifty miles an hour would hit the Willamette Valley. So for this storm, we had a much longer lead time than they had for the 1962 Columbus Day storm."

Though damage was more extensive during the Columbus Day storm (partly because the warning period was so limited), the 1996 windstorm set a new all-time state record for low air pressure—28.51 at Astoria (the previous record of 28.56 dated back to 1880)—and sent winds of 119 miles per hour blowing through the Sea Lion Caves.

Seattle was spared the full brunt of the December 1995 windstorm, but the blow was still a fairly heavy weather event around Puget Sound and a source of major jubilation for local weather forecasters. "It was a triumph," says Cliff Mass proudly, "just a tremendous moment for us. We put out the forecast a day or two before, the media went wild, people took it seriously. We said the winds were going to hit Seattle between 6 and 9 P.M., and that's just when they arrived. People got off work before the event; schools and government offices shut down." Brad Colman at the Seattle forecast office was especially pleased that the media and the public took the forecast seriously, which was not the case with the last major Seattle-area windstorm, the Inauguration Day storm of January 1993. According to Colman, the National Weather Service put up the same warnings for both storms, but in 1993 the media "chose not to listen"—perhaps because they were preoccupied with President Clinton's inauguration. "The word did not get out to the community that time," says Colman, "but it was quite the opposite in December 1995. The forecast was the same, but communication was better. End to end, the whole system worked this time." Such are the joys of weather forecasting in the Pacific Northwest.

Local atmospheric scientists are also forging ahead in their ability to forecast the occasional "outbreaks" of arctic air that burst our water pipes, frost our driveways, and reveal the inadequacies of our home insulation. Again, the region's complex terrain is a factor. Just as the Columbia Gorge occasionally funnels cold continental air into Portland, so the Fraser Gap—the opening in the Cascade Range created by the Fraser River valley in Canada—sometimes brings arctic temperatures, as well as wind and snow, into northwestern Washington. Mass, who collaborated with several colleagues on a paper about the subject, notes that the setup for a Fraser Gap event is high pressure and cold air over the interior of southern British Columbia and low pressure over western Washington. The contrasting areas of air pressure create strong northeast winds that accelerate through the Fraser Gap and funnel down to the San Juan Islands, Guemes Island, Fidalgo Island, and northern Whidbey Island. The Fraser Gap flow is "the most important source of cold, arctic air for the lowlands of western Washington," write Mass and his co-authors, "and is associated with the most significant snow events over the region." On average, these arctic outbreaks occur only once or twice a year, but they seem to be on the upswing, both in frequency and intensity. Certainly the December 28, 1990, storm analyzed in Mass's paper was a humdinger—"the most intense in living memory at most locations," according to "numerous long-term residents." These nameless, numberless longtimers sound suspiciously like the "oldest living settler" who was always being trotted out by newspaper reporters back in the old days to pass judgment on weird weather events. But no matter. A dash of local lore makes science more palatable.

Mass and his co-authors do not speculate about why Fraser Gap arctic outbreaks are becoming more common—but these days, when you read about any unusual weather, there is a strong temptation to link it to greenhouse-induced global climate change. We do seem to be getting a heavy dose of intensely strange weather lately—not just here in the Northwest, but all over the country. Take a look at the record book for the last couple of years: the warmest winter on record in Washington state during 1992–93; record snowfall for a single day in the Cascades in February 1994; record-breaking January warmth in western Washington in 1995; record high temperatures in Seattle in the summer of 1995; record precipitation in Washington and Oregon in the winter of 1995–96; record rainfall in Portland, and second-highest rainfall on record in Seattle, in 1996; record number of days over 90° in Portland in July 1996. And on and on it goes. Is something strange happening to our weather? Are all of these violent meteorological swings somehow related to the greenhouse effect? Are we entering a period not only of unprecedented warmth but also of unprecedented storminess?

The short answer is this: it's still too soon to know for sure. Severe weather is certainly nothing new in the United States, which is blessed and cursed with the most and greatest variety of extreme weather in the world—everything from blizzards to tornadoes, droughts to hurricanes. Even here in the mild, tranquil, temperate Pacific Northwest, wild weather has been a recurring theme throughout our brief history. So a jump in the incidence of windstorms and a series of broken temperature and rainfall records may be part of the natural cycle—just another sign of chaos at work. Maybe—but maybe not. There is some research, still fairly sketchy and speculative, suggesting that, possibly as a result of global warming, the northeast Pacific will see fewer small storms—the typical low pressure systems that blow in one after another during the winter months, bringing intermittent rain showers—but will experience more major "weather events" that tear down trees, knock out power lines, and swell rivers over flood level. This is consistent with recently compiled statistics demonstrating that the classic "nor'easter" storms of America's East Coast have diminished in frequency but increased in strength and destructiveness since the mid-1960s. But again, the reason for the change and its connection with global warming are far from clear. "The outright honest answer is that we don't know," Dr. Robert E. Davis, climatologist at the University of Virginia, told a reporter for the *New York Times*.

What we *do* know with considerably more certainty is that the weather of the Pacific Northwest, in fact of much of the Pacific Rim, is subject to long cyclical swings between a cold-wet regime and a warm-dry regime. John M. Wallace, a professor of atmospheric sciences at the University of Washington and a prominent member of the climatology community, describes some of the groundbreaking research that he and his colleagues at the University of Washington have been pursuing in the past few years:

> This has been a very active area of research here, and the pieces are now fitting together to give us a big picture of what has happened over the last seventy to eighty years, which is about as far as we go back. Relying on historical records of sea surface temperatures, pressure patterns over the Pacific, temperature along the coast, runoff in rivers, fishery records, and winter snowfall, we've concluded that there has been some substantial inter-decadal variability—bigger than you'd expect to happen purely by chance. The swings have been large enough to impact how good fishing is and how good skiing has been, large enough to color

the way people would view the climate of this region, especially in winter.

In broad brush, it appears that the warm-dry/cold-wet cycles alternate every twenty to thirty years. Wallace breaks it down this way:

> From 1977 to as close to the present as we can ascertain reliably, it has been warm and relatively dry in winter, bad for skiing, with lower stream flow and less availability of water. In Alaska, this recent warm-dry regime has been unusually productive for salmon, with record catches and higher stream flows. But for the preceding three decades, from about the mid-1940s through the mid-1970s, we had record-setting snows and some record cold temperatures. Ski area operators were doing well. The period from about 1925 to 1943 was analogous to our recent cycle of warm and dry. Before that it's a little more difficult to make sense of the data.

Wallace notes that the difference in precipitation between cycles is about 20 percent—not enough to wreak environmental havoc, but enough to make a noticeable difference in the weather.

So what lies ahead? Has the warm-dry regime run its course? Are we due for a big change? Wallace cautions that work on the decadal cycles is "just descriptive—it has no predictive value." In a sense, this is a science of hindsight: you can never really tell what pattern you're in until you look back at it several years down the road. As Nick Bond, a research meteorologist with the Pacific Marine Environmental Lab, puts it, "These cycles set up a very slow variation in global circulation patterns. I like to use the analogy of a deck of cards. These slow and large-scale processes stack the deck for small and localized events like individual storms. The big shifts can't be used in forecasting, but they increase the tendency one way or another." Like Wallace, whose work has strongly influenced his thinking, Bond emphasizes how difficult it is to know precisely when the pendulum is changing direction, but he speculates that our current cycle may be coming to an end: "It looks like we may be starting to get out of the warm and dry pattern, at least for a while. We've gotten some cool and wet weather in the early fall [of 1996], and the overall flow pattern suggests that there is a fighting chance for a cold winter." In addition, the ocean temperature in the Gulf of Alaska is good deal colder than it's been for some time—another predictor of a "real" winter here in the Northwest. So should we batten down our hatches? "The next cycle is not necessarily going to be cold and wet," says Bond, "but at least back to near normal. In other words, a fair deck—not stacked one way or another. Of course, you can still get dealt a full house with a fair deck. And, to push the analogy, we don't know how the atmosphere will shuffle the cards until they are dealt." Nathan Mantua, a research associate with the University of Washington's Joint Institute for the Study of the Atmosphere and Ocean who has studied decadal cycles, adds an interesting qualification: "'Normal,' to me, is not *average*. Actually, 'normal' in this region is when the climate is in one of these extreme states." In other words, change is by definition going to mean fairly radical change.

Another key factor in determining what cards go into the atmospheric deck is the phenomenon known as ENSO (El Niño—Southern Oscillation). An ENSO event is a naturally occurring periodic alteration of the ocean-atmosphere interaction in the tropical Pacific. In a "normal" year there is moderate warming of the cold surface waters off Peru around Christmastime, an occurrence that Peruvian fishermen named El Niño, for the Christ child. But when scientists use the term El Niño, they are referring to an unusually pronounced and extensive warming of the surface waters of the equatorial Pacific. El Niños, which occur roughly every two to seven years, set off a kind of chain reaction in the earth's atmosphere: warmer surface waters and weaker trade winds shift the strongest thunderstorm activity to the central Pacific, which in turn allows a strong ridge of high pressure to build over the western Pacific, creating drought conditions in Australia. Here in the Pacific Northwest, El Niño makes late winter and spring warmer and often drier than average, while in the southeastern states, conditions turn wet and cool; California can go either way—very wet or very dry, depending on the position of the jet stream. When the pendulum swings back, a La Niña occurs, with colder than normal tropical waters and cold and often wet winters here in the Northwest. When record-breaking rains hit parts of Washington and Oregon during the winter of 1995–96, many blamed La Niña, but in fact current research shows that there was only a weak to moderate cooling in the tropical Pacific. And even though rainfall in our region was high, temperatures were slightly warmer than normal. "My personal feeling about the winter of 1995–96 is that the tropical Pacific did not have much of an impact on our weather," says Nick Bond. "It was a case of the atmosphere in the Northern Hemisphere doing its own thing."

In the past few years, researchers have made significant headway in understanding both El Niño and the inter-decadal cycles; now they're beginning to tackle the question of whether and how these two patterns are related. "They seem to be connected, but the verdict is still out," says John Wallace. "They do have certain things in common when you look at them year to year and decade to decade. When it's warm in the equatorial Pacific, that goes with colder temperatures in the north and central Pacific, warm temperatures on the American coast, and a deep Aleutian low in the pressure pattern. The real question is whether the mechanism behind El Niño and the inter-decadal cycle is the same. I'm keeping an open mind." Nick Bond notes that causation is tricky to determine with such large and long-term patterns: "We have noticed that since the mid- to late 1970s the tropical Pacific has 'liked' to have warm events—there has been only one significant cold event since then. And this has been a warm-dry period in the Pacific Northwest. But the difficulty is ferreting out cause and effect. We see a connection between El Niño and the decadal cycle, but we don't know which is driving which."

Inevitably, any discussion of climatic cause and effect circles back to the vexed question of global warming. Is it possible that all this warm dry weather we've been having since the late 1970s is *not* part of a natural cycle, whether inter-decadal or El Niño-influenced, but is rather the result of global warming brought on by the rising levels of so-called greenhouse gases in the atmosphere? Wallace, examining the data on inter-decadal variability, does not think so. The fluctuations we've experienced here in the Pacific Northwest, from the warm dry 1920s and 1930s, to the chilly wet late 1940s, 1950s, 1960s and early 1970s, and back to the warm dry 1980s and 1990s, go well beyond anything postulated by global warming theorists. Nathan Mantua's work on the decade-to-decade cycles shows that during the warm and dry spell that started back in the 1920s, temperatures were quite comparable to our current warm cycle; and there is some evidence that these warm interludes go back at least a few centuries. "This cycle has not been driven by greenhouse warming, though it may bias it one way or another," says Mantua. "It looks as if natural variability is stronger than any global warming signal, at least in the Northwest. We've experienced similar warmings earlier in this century and probably in previous centuries." Bond is similarly unpersuaded that greenhouse warming is fueling ENSO events. He acknowledges that part of the reason global temperatures have been so warm in the 1980s and 1990s is due to the frequency of El Niños in this period, but feels that the question of causation remains undecided: "Have increased greenhouse gases helped El Niños form, or have they just formed and raised global temperatures independently of what humans are doing? This is still an open issue. My personal opinion—and it's really no more than that—is that we haven't ever seen the mechanism by which the greenhouse effect could trigger an El Niño. No one has yet proposed a compelling argument for why it should. There is no question that greenhouse gases are increasing; but to my mind there is still no reason to believe that this is causing more El Niños."

Weather science, like the weather itself, goes in cycles. Right now in the research communities, two apparently opposite trends are taking shape simultaneously. On the one hand, there is an increasing focus on the near-term and the local: forecasters are hoping to tell us with greater accuracy and exactness where tomorrow's rain will fall, how hard it will come down, when it will start, and when it will end. On the other hand, a sizable chunk of research money these days goes into long-term, big-picture issues—global warming, climatological patterns and phenomena that unfold over decades or even centuries, the interrelationship of atmosphere and ocean. Pacific Northwest weather buffs are lucky because both of these research areas are peculiarly relevant to our region and both have inspired excellent work by our local scientists. All of the Northwest atmospheric scientists I spoke to pretty much agreed with Cliff Mass's ringing assertion that "we've learned more about local weather conditions in the last ten years than in the previous hundred years." And John Wallace voiced the same optimism about recent advances in climatological research: "We've seen more progress in making sense out of the bigger picture of climatic patterns in the last five years than everything else put together up to that point."

I came away from my conversations with Mass, Wallace, and their colleagues inspired by a kind of onward-and-upward vision of steady progress and infinite perfectibility: We *will* triumph over nature's chaos, we *will* penetrate the mysteries of the atmosphere, we *will* know what the weather is going to do tomorrow, next month, and into the next decade. Then I checked out the local forecast, and I wondered: Are these breakthroughs in atmospheric research translating into practical advances in weather prediction? The answer is yes, but a subtle yes. Already we're seeing greater refinement and precision in the National Weather Service "zone" forecasts—instead of just "cloudy, chance of showers," the forecasts now specify "showers developing mainly north part, with afternoon thunderstorms in the Cascade foothills."

One big current challenge is figuring out how to communicate more precise and refined forecasts in a way that people can understand (and that can be squeezed into extremely tight radio weather "spots"). I've often chuckled to myself over the seemingly infinite gradations of precipitation potential in our local forecasts—everything from "few showers" to "scattered showers," "lingering showers," plain old "showers," "periods of rain," "rain at times," "occasional rain," "rain changing to showers," "rain, heavy at times," "excessive rain," and so on. As Brad Colman of the Seattle forecast office explains, every gradation is linked to a statistical probability of measurable rainfall. The problem is finding language for the percentages that people will understand. According to Colman, the National Weather Service recently abandoned the term "widely scattered showers" when the agency discovered how ambiguous "widely" was: the weather service forecasters meant wide spaces *between* the showers, that is, lots of places getting *no* rainfall, but many people thought they meant scattered over *wide expanses,* that is, more rain falling than just "scattered showers." Percentage forecasts—"chance of rainfall 40 percent"—have also engendered a fair amount of confusion and misinterpretation. In fact, "chance of rainfall 40 percent" means that the forecaster has concluded, based on computer models, local conditions, and previous weather patterns, that there is a 40 percent likelihood that at least .01 inch of rain will accumulate over the next twelve hours at a single point in the forecast zone (in Seattle it's Sea-Tac airport; in Portland it's the National Weather Service office near the airport). It does *not* mean that rain will fall 40 percent of the time or that it will cover 40 percent of the terrain. But try explaining this to a bleary commuter who just wants to know whether to bring a raincoat or sunglasses to work that day.

There are, of course, skeptics who question the cheery optimism of the National Weather Service. Portland's Jack Capell, for one, is not convinced that the agency's much-ballyhooed $4.5 billion modernization program is all that hot:

> They spent a lot of money on Doppler radar and over-
> sold it to the public. All this emphasis on Doppler and
> new satellites is taking away from other areas—from
> surface observations, for example. Now that they're
> switching over to the Automated Surface Observing
> System [ASOS], there is no human observer to report
> on the higher clouds. I like to know if we're getting an
> increasing high cloud layer, and the ASOS sensors
> don't pick this up. We've also lost the weather ships—
> we used to get reports from light ships, but these
> were replaced by buoys, which are frequently out of
> commission. The National Weather Service has been
> claiming for years that they will improve the forecast
> greatly. I remember reading an article back in the
> early 1960s in which they claimed they'd soon be able
> to predict exactly when rainstorms would start and
> stop. But here it is decades later and they still continue
> to miss. Improvement is gradual and slow in coming.

Bob Lynott, a Portland meteorologist who has put in time with both the National Weather Service and KOIN-TV, has gone even further in his criticisms. "Meteorology has come a long way, but forecasting has not improved in 20 years," wrote Lynott in his broadside at the National Weather Service, *The Weather Tomorrow: Why Can't They Get It Right* (1987). Lynott argued that the weather service has become overly reliant on "robotistic" computer-generated forecasts and that most of its staffers are merely marking time; they'll keep their jobs whether their forecasts are right or wrong, and there is no incentive for them to stick their necks out and go against the computer models. "Government, in collusion with the media, has lowered expectations to the point that the public is satisfied with a lot of fluff and fancy visuals about current events," Lynott told a reporter for the *Oregonian* in 1985. "Nobody expects bold forecasting anymore. People don't even realize what they are missing."

Time will tell whether "bold forecasting" will resurge as meteorologists learn to incorporate theoretical and technological breakthroughs into their predictions or whether increasingly powerful computers will clamp a "robotistic" uniformity on what used to be a delicate blend of science and intuition. My guess is that bold weather will always stir up bold forecasts. As long as storms blow in off the Pacific, as long as rainy seasons alternate with dry, as long as our mountains rise up to deflect air masses and wring the moisture out of clouds, there will always be some awestruck person down here working like a demon to figure out why. A demon artist. A demon scientist. In the end, it probably comes down to the same thing.

Winter

I love almost all kinds of weather and I've never minded getting wet, but I have to confess that I find winter in the Northwest a little hard to take. By the time the winter solstice arrives three weeks into December, it has usually been raining on and off for a good three months with no end in sight. Days are dark, nights are long—in Seattle, on the shortest day of the year, the sun is above the horizon for only eight hours and twenty-seven minutes. Every time you tap the barometer, it seems to tumble a few millibars lower. Everything that stays outside for even a couple of hours turns slimy with moisture. Rot creeps up on you, spiders take over the basement. Unprotected wood seems to melt back into the earth like candle wax. Meteorologists have a slightly crisper terminology for what's going on in the atmosphere. "Winter is the season of traveling lows which are frequent and move by in rapid succession," as atmospheric scientist Phil Church put it. "The frontal passage is usually marked by a minor shift in wind direction, a small increase in speed, almost no change of temperature, a little stronger drizzle, and a temporary thickening of the strato-cumulus clouds." It's those frequent traveling lows you have to watch out for. Low barometric pressure does funny things to your brain: makes you groggy and headachy, lethargic and irritable— low-spirited, as they used to say.

The combination of low light, low pressure, and dripping clouds results in a collective regional bummer. "Tremendous rain and hail, full of alarming consequences," an anxious

nineteenth-century weather watcher confided to his diary as
yet another storm blew in off the Pacific. "When was the last
time we *really* saw the sun, I mean a truly sunny day with a
deep blue sky and blazing sunshine all day long?" I demanded
peevishly in my own diary toward the end of the very wet
January of 1996. Two weeks later, on February 9, I wept:
"How many days has it been raining now? Six in all, though
it feels like 600, especially after the last two days of steady
heavy dark dank dripping." To make matters worse, it was
abnormally warm for a good part of the winter, so the mountains didn't really have much snow until mid-January and the
earth had an unwholesome squish to it. The tulip leaves in
our garden started pushing up soon after Christmas, and early
in January the daffodil buds were plainly visible and the witch
hazel was in full bloom. Far from cheering me, the flowers
only added to my malaise as they nodded listlessly in the
steady *drip drip drip.*

People used to call this ailment the winter blues, but now
psychologists have come up with an official clinical name: seasonal affective disorder (SAD). Especially severe in northern
latitudes, SAD symptoms range from sleepiness and heightened craving for starchy foods all the way up to suicidal
depression. It's not just your imagination or a bad attitude:
the weather really *is* getting you down, both physically and
psychologically. SAD is one of the reasons why suicide rates
tend to be higher in the Pacific Northwest than in other parts
of the country—for 1994 (the most recent year on record)
the statistics were 14.2 suicides per 100,000 residents in
Washington and 16.6 per 100,000 in Oregon, compared with
12 per 100,000 in the nation as a whole (perplexingly, the
Rocky Mountain states of Montana, Idaho, Wyoming, Colorado, New Mexico, Arizona, Utah, and Nevada all ranked
higher, with a regional rate of 18.3 suicides per 100,000).

In most cases, SAD fades as spring approaches, but meanwhile, in the depths of winter, the best treatment is increased
exposure to light. Experts advise us to spend time outdoors
no matter what the weather, and to keep our houses brightly
lit or install full-spectrum high-intensity lamps and bask in
the wattage as much as possible.

We also find it heartening to remind ourselves that with
every new day of winter the darkness recedes a bit. Winter
is actually a *brightening* season of lengthening days, and the
worst of it is the onset. This is often the case meteorologically as well. Though January is statistically the coldest month
of the year in the Northwest, with average minimum temperatures of 36.1° in Seattle and 33.6° in Portland, December is
often wetter. By February, the heaviest rain is usually over and
average daytime highs have reached 50° west of the Cascades.

Yes, winter is damp and gray, but most of the time the
weather is not nearly as bad or monotonous as we make it
out to be. I was delighted, while reading journalist Charles
Prosch's book, to stumble upon his account of a "cultured
and sensible lady" of the last century who, upon moving to
Olympia in the 1860s, had heard "so many conflicting and
exaggerated reports of the winter rains" that she decided
to find out the truth for herself. She kept a faithful weather
diary all winter, recording each morning and evening the
condition of the weather. Prosch proudly revealed the results
of her foray into climatology: "It had been an ordinary winter,
with the usual amount of rain. This lady's diary showed that
there had actually been more sunny than rainy days during
that 'horribly wet winter,' as many others termed it. And so
it is with our most disagreeable winters; they are never so
bad as some people imagine them to be."

Reviewing my own faithful weather journal, I see that even
the winter of 1995–96, the wettest on record in western

Washington, was not unrelieved horror. "Rainy season is taking a breather right now," begins my entry for December 21, "though we certainly got hit in November with over 10 inches of rain and some of the worst flooding in history along certain rivers. Barely a day went by without some rain. Yet the odd thing is, most of the time it wasn't raining at all. It was either gearing up to rain or recovering from rain. Lots of buildup, little actual time raining, and relatively little hard rain. Even on some of the worst days we had breaks when *whoosh,* a bright damp springlike sun would shine through." The week before Christmas a "blocking high" steered the storms away from us, and we had cloudless skies day after day with frosty nights and mild afternoons. At the end of January and five days into February another clear spell set in, though this time it was brisk, cold, and crystalline with daytime highs only in the 30s. By February 16 I was all but singing: "One solid week of gorgeous, cloudless or almost entirely cloudless, and monotonously identical weather— daytime highs in the upper 50s and low 60s; cool nights in the upper 30s to low 40s. Warm dry May-like afternoons, with temperatures cresting around 3 P.M. or so, then cooling off suddenly after spectacular salmon, iridescent orange, burning coral sunsets. One week of this and one entirely forgets that there could be any other sort of weather."

Fortified by the sun, I decided to spend a weekend in the Olympic rain forest in mid-February to see if it was really as wet as it was cracked up to be. I was not disappointed. Back home, with the contents of my suitcase in the dryer, I wrote in my journal:

> It's the constant dripping that is most remarkable
> about the rain forest. In most of the heavily forested
> areas I've been in, the trees act as umbrellas so that

light rain hardly penetrates the canopy. But here it's
the opposite: even when it stops raining (as I think
it did for a few minutes every now and then, though
it was hard to tell), the drips continue. Everything
is wet and dripping and soaking and gurgling and
seeping water. The gray swirls and opens, lightens,
darkens, coalesces in rain. The moss holds and weeps
out water. Dripping tendrils like green mermaid hair.
The incredible sensation of looking skyward and
feeling/seeing a tiny globe of water fall straight down
from the topmost branch of a 100-foot Sitka spruce,
round and wet and perfect, and land *splat* on one's
nose. The rivers roar, yet aside from that noise and
the whisper of dripping, it is silent: barely any wind
to interrupt the flow of tree and air. And the rain the
rain the rain. Given the forecast, I expected deluging
downpours, but instead we got bands of showers
ranging from light to medium. What amazed me most
was how they came and went and came again: it was a
light, changeable, evanescent, fleeting, magical kind of
misty rain. You'd see the puddles sparkling and dancing
and go in for your raincoat; you'd come back out and
it would barely be drizzling. You'd emerge from the
dripping trees into an open field where it was raining
steadily and wetly; then it would cease altogether for a
moment or two, the sun would swirl darkly behind
the clouds, you'd see a paler patch suggesting blue sky
and clarity, and then another batch of rain would roam
through. Quite beautiful and mystical in its way, but
you come to feel very shut in and fundamentally
mossy after a while. Those enormous towering trees,
however, just seem to soak it up.

For the record book: Quinault, a town and ranger station in the middle of the rain forest, got 173.1 inches
of rain in 1995. Its annual average rainfall, I believe, is
somewhere in the vicinity of 140 inches; some years it
gets 200. But who's counting?

On the way home we made a detour out to the ocean
beach. It was a real Lewis and Clark–style winter day,
wind blowing hard and raw out of the southwest, rain
arriving in gusts, waves all whipped up with foam
blown off in the stiff wind. Severe; forbidding; stormy.
You feel a sense of connection here with all those vast
Pacific weather systems, the pelting rain of California,
the pineapple express, the parade of lows, the incredible blowing immensity of it. The openness of the coast
is a relief after the dense wet green curtained forest,
and it's bracing and glorious to get the wind and the
whipping weather full in your face. But it's also ter-
rible and unsheltered. As the wind stormed without
ceasing and the rain came in bands, I thought of Drake
and Cook and Vancouver, and I well understood how
Cook missed the straits in foul weather and also why
he was scared to get too close to shore for fear of being
stranded. How would you ever get off again, assuming
you survived a shipwreck? In foul weather this is
indeed a frightening savage wet coastline.

From Sunday to Tuesday on the peninsula, we had one
unshrouded ray of sun, which unfortunately fell on a
wasteland of clear-cuts between rain forest and
shore—sun on devastation.

Now, back in Seattle, the sky at 3 P.M. is a shade
darker, can't see the Sound at all, the puddles are
shimmering just a bit. Another band of rain?

And so it goes. The "cultured and sensible lady" from
Olympia and I are in good company with our winter weather
diaries, as I discovered in reading *Winter Brothers,* novelist
Ivan Doig's vivid, far-ranging meditation on the diaries of
nineteenth-century adventurer James Gilchrist Swan. Swan,
a Bostonian who spent the second half of the nineteenth century soaking up the raw, edge-of-the world atmosphere on
Washington's outer coast, recorded many memorable storms
and restorative calms. But Doig's own journal, written in the
course of the winter of 1978–79 and interleaved with Swan's
diary, makes for even better reading, especially in his musings
on the variability of Northwest winter weather. Fifteen days
into winter Doig recorded a magical spell of cold clarity in
Seattle—a rainless glimmering interlude of "identically keen,
tingling" days: "Through yesterday morning the temperature
hung below freezing for four days and nights in a row, the
longest skein of its kind I can remember here at the rim of
the Sound." On day forty-eight (early February) Doig took
stock of the elements again, this time limning more typical
winter fare: "Rain trotting in the drainpipe when we woke
up. Now, at ten in the morning, a gray pause has curtained
between showers, a halfhearted wind musses among the trees.
Today and yesterday are standard Puget Sound winter, rain
and forty-five degrees, after the weeks of clear frost-rimed
weather. A rich winter of two seasons, this. Time of frost,
time of cloud."

Those who have tracked the history of Northwest winters
might contest Doig's assertion that "standard" is "rain and
forty-five degrees"—for there have been many seasons when

anything but prevailed. Steve Mierzejewski provided abundant
evidence of radical departures from the standard in his study
Footprints on the Rivers, in which he painstakingly reconstructed
Northwest winters during the period of exploration and early
settlement. Far from being mild, gentle, and monotonous,
"the Pacific Northwest has as many extreme conditions as any
region," Mierzejewski asserted. But nobody has ever believed
it, so deeply lodged is our reputation for tepid winters. As
Mierzejewski wrote, "It was a long time before anyone dared
to admit that cold spells were an integral part of the Pacific
Northwest's climate. When outbreaks of cold were witnessed
by early settlers it was often spoken of as if it were some
bizarre, never before seen or to be seen again, phenomenon."
"This climate of Oregon is anything but what it has been rep-
resented," Olympia pioneer Zebulon C. Bishop griped to his
brother on January 12, 1850, a year that brought an especially
severe winter. "So far as the Snow seldom falling and when it
does never laying on the ground but melting as fast as it fell I
saw it fall to the depth of a foot and lay[,] while on the
Willamette one hundred and fifty miles further south it was
two feet and the Columbia froze over hard. . . ." On January
25 Bishop added, "Since writting the Snow has fallen to the
depth of three feet and Still Snowing. The weather is
extremely cold so much so as to make ice on the Bay."

According to Mierzejewski, the winter of 1832–33 was
a frigid one, with the Columbia frozen even at Portland for
four weeks; the early 1840s were also cold in the Northwest,
and severe winter weather returned in 1846–47 and 1849
and hung on until 1857. In 1854, Oregonians could ice-skate
on the Willamette from Portland to Oregon City, and snow
was so deep and enduring that sleigh riding became all the
rage. On December 29, 1855, the temperature dropped to
9° in Oregon City and the editor of the local *Argus* wrote,

"Everybody seemed to suffer as much with the cold as they used to in Michigan when the mercury stood at 25 degrees below zero. . . . The most incorrigible old sinners who have hitherto been grumbling at the 'mist,' are now on their knees praying for rain." January 1857 commenced with two feet of snow on the ground in Portland, and there were heavy snow and freezing temperatures again later in the month. The *Oregonian* ran this letter near winter's end: "Sir:—I arrived here yesterday. On picking up your paper, I saw a notice, stating that I had frozen to death on my way from Walla Walla. This is a mistake; I am still living. . . ."

The climax of this run of bitter winters came in 1861–62, which brought early snow, followed by floods, followed by a cold spell that endured for weeks on end. East of the Cascades, as discussed in Chapter Three, this was the most devastating cow-killer winter in history, with heavy snowfall and temperatures as low as 31 below zero decimating cattle herds. But suffering was also intense and widespread west of the mountains. The mean temperature at Vancouver, Washington, in January 1862 was 21.3°, and in Portland rain fell on top of deep snow, collapsing scores of buildings. Portlanders found the arctic January temperatures especially brutal since many residents had lost their homes in the December floods. In Seattle, Arthur Denny's thermometer fell to 2 below zero ("I have never known it lower than that at any time"), Lake Union froze solid six inches down, and snow drifted to two feet. "We now know that any winter may offer a snow storm of two months duration," the Salem *Statesman* declared on January 24, 1862. "We have experienced a duration of snow and a degree of cold, without precedent in the history of the country." The editor of the Oregon City *Argus* remarked philosophically that this winter brought "extremes enough, if reasonably divided, to season a dozen winters." The only benefit was the sleighing—100 days of it in western Washington. The winter of 1861–62 saved its final blow for the eve of summer: on June 12, melting snowpack flooded the Willamette, which sent two feet of water surging over Portland's Front Street.

In the twentieth century we haven't seen a winter to rival 1861–62, but we have set new records for snow depth and cold temperatures. During three days in 1916, from mid-morning January 31 to late afternoon February 2, it snowed without ceasing in Seattle, dumping down 32.5 inches. The heavy wet snow snapped trees and collapsed the dome of St. James Cathedral. Total Seattle snowfall that winter was 60.9 inches—topped in 1968–69 when 67.5 inches accumulated. Longtime Portland weathercaster Jack Capell recalls that the winter of 1968–69 was the only time he missed a news show due to weather: "During one January storm that winter the temperature did not rise above 8° at the airport, and winds reached 50 to 60 knots. The wind was so strong and came up so suddenly that a couple of hunters got stranded on one of the river islands, and they could not figure out how to get them off. One hunter died. Since I couldn't get out of my driveway, the television station sent a car, which for some reason dropped me at the airport. That was a mistake—I was stranded by the storm." Another memorable winter west of the mountains was 1950, when temperatures sank to a record low of 0° on January 31 at Sea-Tac airport and a record 3 below zero in February at the Portland airport; Sea-Tac racked up 57.2 inches of snow that January, and thirteen people died in a single blizzard in Seattle (Portland hit its daily snow record seven years earlier on January 21, 1943, when 15.5 inches fell on downtown).

These lowland snowfall figures pale, of course, when set
beside the awesome depths that pile up in the mountains:
during the winter of 1971–72, Mount Rainier's Paradise
Ranger Station (elevation 5,500 feet) measured 1,122 inches
of snow. And in 1994 Mount Rainier set a national twenty-
four-hour snowfall record when more than 70 inches fell
from February 23 to 24. Rapid accumulations of deep snow
bring joy to skiers and water managers, but they also raise
the risk of avalanches. Mountain snowpacks become unstable
when temperatures fluctuate: the snow melts, becomes saturated with water, and refreezes when temperatures drop; the
fresh snow that falls on top of the frozen crust is extremely
precarious, especially when it gets wet and heavy. One of the
most disastrous avalanches in Washington history occurred
in the Cascades under just these conditions in March 1910.
A January thaw melted a heavy snowpack up to 7,000 feet,
and then the wet snow crusted over. February brought a huge
accumulation of snow, with 180 inches falling on Snoqualmie
Pass between February 21 and 28. On March 1, two trains
stranded up in Stevens Pass were tumbled into a canyon and
buried after a heavy rain sent tons of snow sliding down the
steep mountain slope above. Ninety-six people died in the
wreckage; there were only twenty-two survivors, several of
them seriously injured.

Avalanches dislodge snow; the warm wind known as the
chinook consumes it. Named for a Native American tribe that
once occupied the coastal areas north of the Columbia River,
the chinook is a southwest winter wind that carries tropical
air from the equatorial Pacific up to the Pacific Northwest.
As George W. Fuller explains in *A History of the Pacific Northwest* (1949), a chinook brings rain to the regions west of the
Cascades, but "it penetrates to the interior . . . robbed of its
moisture, and its warm breath often causes a blanket of snow

to disappear from the ground in a few hours." Hence the other name for the wind—the snow-eater. Narcissa Whitman, who died with her missionary husband, Dr. Marcus Whitman, in a notorious Indian massacre near Walla Walla in November 1847, sent her parents a letter about a chinook wind that blew through eastern Washington in the last days of 1837. The warm wind melted the deep snow of the Blue Mountains, and the runoff flooded the Walla Walla River. As Narcissa wrote, the rising river waters were threatening to undermine their house: "On the eve of the 28th [of December] the waters entered our cellar, the walls settled, the props gave away one after another, & for the whole night we were in the utmost anxiety, fearing the consequences to our whole house."

Sadly for snow-lovers, there really hasn't been a "good" winter west of the Cascades since 1969. "Snowfall has gone down significantly in recent years," notes Brad Colman of the National Weather Service forecast office in Seattle. "The thirty-year average has dropped 10 percent." Global warming? Maybe not. Recent studies indicate that Northwest winters are governed by decadal cycles of cold-wet alternating with warm-dry (as discussed in Chapter Four). Some weather scientists believe we are now emerging from a prolonged warm-dry cycle and heading into cold-wet. As Oregon state climatologist George H. Taylor remarked after the torrential downpours, heavy mountain snows, and floods of the winter of 1995–96: "There are a lot of people who have not seen a normal winter in Oregon, and now we're seeing it. We may have been lulled into a false sense of security and may see more of these in the next decade than we've seen."

The winter of 1996–97 certainly was a doozy, with storm after storm hitting southern Oregon in mid-December, a ten-foot pre-Christmas base at many Northwest ski areas, and 7

inches of snow in Seattle in November. Then, to cap it off,
came the incredible week after Christmas: 18 inches of snow
falling on the Seattle National Weather Service forecast office
at Sand Point between December 26 and 29, followed by 3.69
inches of rain from December 30 to January 2. Temperatures
swung from a low of 26° to a record-breaking high of 55°
during the period. The result: region-wide flooding and hundreds of millions of dollars of damage to homes, farms, and
businesses as roofs and carports caved in, sinkholes opened in
roads, and mud slides slammed into living rooms. Twenty-
four people died in Washington as a result of the winter
storms: the eruption of Mount St. Helens was the only
regional natural disaster to take more lives. Preliminary
damage estimates have already reached $160 million and are
expected to go much higher once all the figures from home-
owners are tallied.

I can proudly say I lived through the holiday storms of
1996–97. My weather journal conveys some of the ecstasy
and agony that convulsed western Washington:

> December 27: *The blizzard of '96!!!!!* By late morning
> yesterday, the drizzle of freezing rain had turned to
> heavy freezing rain, then to hard glorious fluffy snow,
> and by early afternoon it was really coming down in
> swans' feathers, turning the air and the world into
> general solid white. We had off-and-on snow and
> freezing rain until late at night, when it all turned
> to snow, and it was still snowing when we woke up
> this morning. Here, north of the city, we got over a
> foot; Seattle got 9 inches to a foot; Bellingham more.
> Wow. Temperatures held steady in the mid- to upper
> 20s. Portland got rain and freezing rain, with much
> warmer temps. Incredibly beautiful. Spent the morning

sledding down our own hill, still unplowed. A few
flurries fell around 10 A.M., now trying to clear, the
Sound is once again visible. We were lucky because
for much of yesterday areas to the south, like Kent,
got mostly freezing rain. That clattering horror.
Winter wonderland. Passes closed. Good thing we
didn't try to go skiing.

December 30: *The great slushfest*. Blizzard was one
thing; slush is quite another. Here's the lowdown:
Friday night it started snowing again around 8 P.M.
or so, nice and light and pretty, with temps holding
in upper 20s to low 30s. Snowed all night, getting
gradually heavier, and by 5 A.M. it looked like maybe
6 to 8 inches on top of the 12 to 14 inches already
on the ground. A gorgeous New England scene. But
wait. By 6 A.M. the snow had turned to rain, temps
had risen into mid-30s; and it rained all day, miserably
cold, wet, nasty rain. All the 18 or so inches of snow
turned to cement, a dirty lumpy glop. When you
stepped out in it, your foot would sink down to a layer
of murky slush that looked like broken opaque glass,
the kind they put on bathroom windows. The snow
deflating fast like a three-day-old party balloon. We
noticed a fairly serious crack in the paint on one of
our walls—no water leaking in, but apparently the
column next to it has buckled or shifted somewhat. I
went up on the roof to shovel, fearing that the weight
of the snow would collapse the house. It was a horror
getting the slush off; downspouts clogged and frozen
so a lot of the standing water under the snow was not
draining off. The low point was when I finally got a
downspout cleared by reaching up and yanking off the

elbow, and this load of slush ran right down my sleeve and down my back. Rain kept up pretty much all day; temps warmed a lot and got into 40s at some point. Wind blew like crazy, a chinook wind; clouds cleared off, but it kept on warming. Raining again when we got up this morning. It stopped by late morning, but it's supposed to rain more off and on all week. Rivers flooding all over the state. Passes closed. Snow levels keep rising. A super complete mess. Yuck. This has certainly been a memorable stretch of weather with which to close out the year.

When all was said and done, 1996–97 did not rival 1968–69 for snow accumulation west of the Cascades, but it was indeed a winter to remember.

The occasional sparkle of snow is not the only consolation of a Northwest winter. A lot of folks complain about how short our summers are—but so are the winters. In some years they're over before they actually start. Flowers, if you look for them, bloom all year; and by late January and early February you don't have to look for them—witch hazel (*Hamamelis mollis*), various kinds of hellebore, sweetly fragrant *Daphne odora,* and early species of *Erica* (commonly known as heath) are everywhere. Mild spells in December, January, and February bring out the delicate, pale pink flowers of the *Prunus subhirtella* 'Autumnalis,' an ornamental cherry tree widely grown west of the Cascades. I love telling snowbound friends and family back East about our January crocuses and February daffodils and camellias that riot with color in midwinter. We also have the freedom here to choose winter when we want it: the mountainous terrain lets us switch seasonal backdrops in a couple of hours. Even after several

winters here, the ritual weekend trek to the ski slopes still
thrills me: the morning departure in the gray drizzle, the
sleety swelling of raindrops as you approach the snow line,
the miraculous changeover from dark dirty rain to clean
white snow, the slow slippery drive through the wonderland
of snow-laden firs, the snowpacked mountain flanks, bright
even in the dullest weather, and, after a day of whirling flakes,
the welcome return to the moist green of Puget Sound.
There was a Saturday last winter when I left Snoqualmie Pass
after skiing all day in heavy snow, descended into heavy rain
around Fall City, and then, as I approached Seattle, drove into
dazzling sunshine; the cloud just ended like a cliff dropping
off—driving rain and snow on one side, sun on the other. My
car still had scraps of snow on it, water vapor was steaming
off the hood, and there I was reaching for my sunglasses. The
next day, despite a forecast of scattered showers, we woke
up to a light cottony snowfall that floated through the air
until sundown. Two inches, gone without a trace by Monday
morning.

In winter, when the sun rides low in the sky and appears
only at long intervals in "bursts" and "breaks," you really
notice the light. Sunbeams steal into places where you've
never seen them before, searching out odd cracks and corners. Shadows turn a deep velvet. South-facing walls create
transitory micro-summers in the short afternoons. "Feath-
ered, happy light," Sallie Tisdale has called the fleeting clarity
of early January, "like elf light, lightweight, light light. All
the fat is trimmed away: all the leaves and green, the growth,
the aromas and moisture and heat."

"The steeper the trough, the faster the climb," a friend
of mine is fond of saying about the relationship between latitude and the hours of daylight. The light that drains away so
alarmingly in October and November comes back to us in a

brightening flood in February and March. Afternoons lengthen. Storms diminish in intensity and frequency. Even when it's raining, the air somehow feels lighter and cleaner— like a curtain of gauze instead of the dirty, tattered drapes of December. The sun of late winter is warm on your face. The wind no longer smells of fog and rotting leaves. The mud is starting to crumble. By the vernal equinox, blessed of name, it's official; but it usually feels like spring well before that. As March melts into its third week, you can pat yourself on the back and smile. Congratulations, you've survived another Northwest winter.

Chapter Five

"The rain!
The rain!
My God, the rain!"

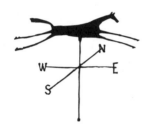

WRITERS'
WEATHER

WEATHER IN LITERATURE IS mostly awful—symbolically stormy, disastrously droughty, suspensefully strange, unbearably hot, or just plain dismal. The Pacific Northwest, naturally, has some of the foulest weather in American letters. What writer could resist capitalizing on the region's reputation for damp misery? "I had every intention of dispelling the Pacific Northwest's reputation for rain," wrote Bruce Barcott of his labors in compiling a regional literary anthology. "But I cannot deny the evidence. It rained everywhere." Partly cloudy, chance of showers—that quintessential Northwest forecast—just doesn't "play" in literature. No matter what the weather was doing at the time of composition, it really does rain just about all the time in Northwest fiction—or it ceases to rain with such a vengeance that the wheat fails, the earth cracks, and clouds of dust billow through the air. Ours is a literature of meteorological extremity. But fortunately not monotony. In the stories, novels, poems, and memoirs of this place, weather—particularly, wet weather—comes in all guises and rouses all manner of emotion, from weariness to resignation to euphoria to suicidal despair to cosmic transcendence to serene acceptance. Weather is not mere background or peripheral mood-setting device: some of the most emotional, beautiful, deeply charged, vividly realized, spiritually climactic moments in our literature are about or determined by weather. If ever one needed proof of how profoundly we are influenced, inspired, oppressed, and exhilarated by the weather of the Pacific Northwest, it is here in our literature. "The good rain," to borrow the title of a popular book by Seattle journalist Timothy Egan, has kept our writers going for quite some time, and it shows no sign of letting up.

It may sound presumptuous to speak of literary tradition in a region whose literature dates back scarcely more than a century—but certainly our writers have worked hard and fast to put the Pacific Northwest on America's literary map. Early on, weather—especially big, oppressive, spirit-crushing, grandly horrible weather—emerged as a defining regional literary conceit, rather like grotesquerie and madness in the South. While incestuous siblings, crazed beauticians, and bellowing half-wits parade through the fictions of the Deep South, we get floods, suicidal sunless winters, and punishingly low barometric pressure. Call it meteorological gothic. At the head of this Northwest school of gruesome literary weather stands Harold Lenoir Davis, who published as H. L. Davis. He was one of the first serious

Pacific Northwest writers to make the region, and its climate, not only the *backdrop* but also the *subject* of his work. Born in the Cascade foothills in 1894 and transplanted at age fourteen to the dry landscapes of The Dalles on the Columbia River, Davis was ambitious on a grand scale—the kind of scale that looks attainable only at the founding of empires or the plowing up of virgin soil. Having complained in the early 1930s of the literary bilge spewing forth from the Northwest, he set out to reverse the tide single-handedly in his first novel, *Honey in the Horn,* published in 1935. This sprawling, muscular Oregonian saga impressed the New York literary critics and pundits mightily: *Honey in the Horn* won both the Pulitzer Prize and the Harper Award—no mean feat for a unknown scribbler from the hinterlands.

Davis's hero, Clay Calvert, is appealingly and appallingly rough-hewn—a youthful jailbreaker with "a knob-jointed godforsakenness of expression about him," an orphan and a knockabout intent on finding a place for himself in a hostile, hardworking proletarian world. Clay's wanderings expose him to a wide cross section of early twentieth-century Oregon life—as Davis stated in the book's prefatory note, he "had originally hoped to include in the book a representative of every calling that existed in the State of Oregon during the homesteading period—1906-1908." And so we get portraits of sheepherders, horse traders, loggers, homesteaders, migrant "crop followers" and hay cutters, sawmill operators, and even an oddball writer-historian named Uncle Preston Shiveley, the scholar of Shoestring Valley, whose literary endeavors had never "brought him in the worth of a mule's heel full of hay." Along the way, Davis also serves up several thick slices of Oregon weather—most of it fabulously awful. Not ten pages into the novel, Uncle Preston gets seriously distracted from his labor on a history of Oregon's early statues by "a fierce flood of early rain" that "drowned the country, hoisted the river clear up to the toll-bridge deck-planks, and caught all his sheep to hellan-gone in the mountains with only about a nine-to-eleven chance of getting out." Davis's prose fairly brims with wetness:

> Even to a country accustomed to rain, that was a
> storm worth gawking at. It cracked shingles in the
> roof, loaded the full-fruited old apple-trees until
> they threatened to split apart, and beat the roads
> under water belly-deep to a horse. Ten-foot walls of
> spray went marching back and forth across the hay-
> meadow as if they owned it, flocks of wild ducks came
> squalling down to roost in the open pasture till the air
> cleared, and the river boiled yellow foam over the
> toll bridge stumps, fence rails, pieces of old houses,
> and carcasses of drowned calves and horses against it.

As the rain pours down, Clay gets stuck with the job of trying to herd a flock of sheep out of the mountains and across flooded open countryside to a stack-yard corral, a labor that turns Herculean when the exhausted animals decide to commit suicide by plunging into the floodwaters. Eventually, by sheer force of cussedness and "jesusly hard work," Clay manages to haul, wrestle, and butt the greater part of the "cold, slimy" herd onto dry land, but he nearly dissolves in the process: "He was loose ribbed and logy, and there was no more life in his muscles than in a cut of wet rope. . . . Even to a country accustomed to rain," as Davis wrote, it doesn't get much wetter than this.

Or maybe it does. A few hundred pages later, Clay and his girl-friend, Luce, hole up in an oceanfront cabin and together wait out an entire winter of Pacific storms:

> There were a few weeks in October when the days
> were warm and still, when leaves browned and grass
> ripened in the sun and the reflection of light from
> the sea lasted until long after nightfall, as if the sun
> from some distant stand was shining back at them
> through the transparent curve of water. Afterwards
> the sky blackened and snow fell, and from that time
> until spring the rain never totally stopped and the
> light never entirely started. Except on the line of surf,
> the sea itself was like ink, and the tremendous winds
> that blew out of it carried fierce twisters of rain that
> turned everything pitchy as they passed.

Shades of Lewis and Clark!

Winter's dark, wet oppression clearly fired Davis's imagination, and he continues with a wonderfully apt description of seasonal affective disorder (a term that had yet to be coined):

> That was the time that wore people's nerves the
> hardest. Old squatters from the creek canyons
> bucked mud and wet brush and risked rheumatism
> for the sake of somebody to talk to, when all the
> good they got out of visits was to pick quarrels and
> flounce back home to their heart-eating loneliness
> again. Even the Indians in the river village turned
> short-tempered, though they had had around forty
> generations of continuous residence to get accustomed
> to the climate. The horse-trader and his wife lost flesh
> and color, squabbled incessantly, and split the blankets
> and whacked up the cooking-utensils to separate

permanently at least once a week. No play-parties or
dances went on, because people who had lived that
season out before knew there was no use trying to
improve or lighten it.

Clay actually welcomes the winter wet because the mud and
rain keep his pursuers away. Several plot twists later, he more or
less clears his name, makes up with his girlfriend, and shows signs
of settling down at last.

Honey in the Horn has a grim, squint-eyed, chin-jutted swagger
that feels dated and forced today. Though it's set in the first
decade of the century, this is unmistakably a Depression-era novel
in which social and economic issues take precedence over psy-
chology, character development, emotion, or wit. The same
political agenda informs the book's weather. Whether it's shingle-
warping rain or starve-out dust bowl drought, this is the weather
of poverty.

Davis's weather was fantastically wretched but grounded in the
credible: those wet, death-wishing sheep have the ring of truth,
even if the truth is stretched for effect. In the tall tales told by a
Rogue River mail carrier named Hathaway Jones, bad weather
floats free of reality like an unballasted hot-air balloon. A fabled
and self-proclaimed liar, the son and grandson of liars, Hathaway
Jones told his stories to anyone who would stop to listen to him
as he made the rounds of his wild and woolly mail route in southwest Oregon from 1898 to 1937. Jones yarned about anything
and everything, from feats of amazing endurance to animal
stunts; inevitably, some of the tales revolved around the unbelievable weather to which the Rogue River district is prone.

"Some winters it would rain ceaselessly for months," he recounted in his best deadpan manner in one tale, "not just ordinary rain, but torrential downpours. The trail would be covered for miles with landslides, and even where it was clear, the pack mules would sink almost to their bellies into the mud and slush. Those were the winters Hathaway called mild." (When the tales got recorded, Jones spoke of himself in the third person.) There were even taller tales about the unmild winters when the prodigious precipitation came down as snow instead of rain, transforming the landscape in remarkable ways. In a winter tale called "The Remarkable Watch," Jones claimed that he had lost his watch in the snow in the middle of one incredibly snowy winter and found it the next spring, hanging from a tree branch sixty feet up. (Actually, sixty feet of snow in the Cascades is no tall tale. The winter of 1996–97, Paradise on Mount Rainier measured a cumulative snowfall approaching seventy-eight feet.)

Scholars place Hathaway Jones in the tradition of the eighteenth-century German Baron von Münchhausen, who elaborated his military exploits in the wars against Ottoman Turks into "marvelous narratives"—that is, lies. The comparison may be justified as far as *form* goes; but in terms of *content,* especially meteorological content, I'd lump Jones in with H. L. Davis as a grandiose griper. They certainly weren't pluvial celebrants (those would come later) or precipitation apologists, but they *were* amazed and abashed and, in Jones's case, amused witnesses to how wet it can get out here.

The same note, in a slightly different key, is sounded in Betty MacDonald's 1945 bestseller *The Egg and I,* a semifictional memoir about her misadventures on a chicken ranch situated at the fringes of the Olympic rain forest. Man oh man, did it ever pour on her:

> It rained and rained and rained and rained. It driz-zled—misted—drooled—spat—poured—and just plain rained. Some mornings were black and wild, with a storm raging in and out and around the mountains. Rain was driven under the doors and down the chimney, and Bob [her husband] went to the chicken house swathed in oilskins like a Newfoundland fisherman and I huddled by the stove and brooded about inside toilets. Other days were just gray and low hanging with a continual pit-pat-pit-pat-pitta-patta-pitta-patta which became as vexing as listening to baby talk. Along about November I began to forget when it hadn't been raining and became as one with all the characters in all of the novels about rainy seasons, who rush around banging their heads against the walls, drinking water glasses of straight whiskey and moaning, "The rain! The rain! My God, the rain!"

Betty MacDonald is a weather victim. She is also quite funny: she is the butt of her own jokes, and more often than not, Northwest weather is the punch line. Chatty, endearing, comically exaggerated (or maybe not so exaggerated), *The Egg and I* puts a silly spin on the horror of winter wet. Where Davis grits and Jones distorts, MacDonald grins. But all three share the same underlying assumption: The weather here stinks, and if you live here long enough the stink will creep its way into the very center of your soul.

I came across a wonderful recent variation on this weather victim theme in the title poem of a 1979 collection by Colleen

J. McElroy—"Winters Without Snow." In just three words, McElroy captures the essence of the long, dreary, undramatic winters of western Washington and Oregon. A poet, speech therapist, and creative writing teacher who left the Midwest (St. Louis and Kansas) in the mid-1960s for Bellingham and then Seattle, McElroy devoted most of the poems in this volume to love, birth, loneliness, death, and the multiple dislocations of being black and female in America. But in "Winters Without Snow" she sinks deep down into the misery of muddling through yet another Northwest rainy season:

> Under the grey smother of clouds,
> The layers of grey upon grey,
> Mist rolls against earth
> Like unwound spools of ribbon
> For a shroud.

The air is so dense with moisture it swallows everything solid: "There is no earth. . . . / Even brick and stone fade. . . . / The only signs of life are the swish of rubber / As tires cut across wet pavement." The dull thud of the cadence; the languor of lines that trail off without resolution; the unyielding, uniform gray: everything conjures up the winter depression that will not lift, that goes on and on like the wet days with no change, no denouement, no climax. "You turn inward, broiling against thunderheads / That never come to full steam." Yet "Winters Without Snow" paradoxically defeats the bad mood it so deftly delineates, since the very act of composition requires a summoning of energy and focus and perspective that breaks the spell of depression.

"The rain! The rain! My God, the rain!" This is the bass note, the deep background, the first premise of all Northwest imaginative literature. Over the years, there have been plenty of denials, departures, qualifications, new perspectives, revisions, and revisitations, but this seeping damp horror is the universal point of departure. If you live here and write about it, you have to confront the wet sooner or later. There is no escaping it.

Unless, of course, you slip over the Cascades and escape to an altogether different climate. What wet and dark are to the literature of the *west* Northwest, heat and drought are to the *east*. In many of the novels and stories set on the dry side, especially the agricultural fictions, lack of rain takes center stage as prime plot mover, suspense creator, or parched villain. One of the driest books I came across was *The Desert of Wheat* (1919) by Zane Grey, the granddaddy of that great American literary genre known as the Western. A native of Zanesville, Ohio, Grey cannot be claimed as a Pacific Northwest writer, for he never really lived in these parts; but he did spend enough time out here during his extensive Western travels from 1907 through 1918 to get a feel for the weather in the arid country east of the Cascades, and he used this country as the backdrop for several of his novels. *The Desert of Wheat,* though saddled with a leaden anti-German, anti-Wobbly plot inspired by America's entry into the First World War, contains some of the most crackling descriptions of heat, drought, and the blessed relief of rain in our literature. Grey opens the book with a cinematic pan over the "heroic" land, the cloudless sky, and the pitiless weather that make the West the West:

> A lovely, hard, heroic country, where flowers and
> fruit were not, nor birds and brooks, nor green pas-
> tures. Whirling strings of dust looped up over fallow

ground, the short, dry wheat lay back from the wind,
the haze in the distance was drab and smoky, heavy
with substance.

. . . The sun shone hot, the wind blew hard, and over
the boundless undulating expanse hovered a shadow
that was neither hood of dust nor hue of gold. It was
not physical, but lonely, waiting, prophetic, and weird.
. . . Strange and unfathomable that so much of the
bread of man, the staff of life, the hope of civilization
in this tragic year 1917, should come from a vast,
treeless, waterless, dreary desert!

The eastern Washington desert is even vaster and stranger and
drearier than usual as the novel begins, for a prolonged drought
accompanied by "the most torrid spell on record" has set in,
threatening to destroy the precious wheat harvest: "The haze of
heat seemed like a pall of thin smoke from distant forest fires. The
sun rose, a great, pale-red ball, hot at sunrise, and it soared
blazing-white at noon, to burn slowly westward through a cloudless coppery sky, at last to set sullen and crimson over the ranges."

As *The Desert of Wheat* lumbers on, the drought eventually
breaks, the wheat harvest is mostly saved, the Wobblies are pun-
ished for their dastardly plot to burn the wheat fields, and the
handsome young German-American wheat farmer proves his
patriotic mettle by defying his cranky German father and
marching off to fight in France; he is rewarded for his daring with
marriage to the woman he loves, whose daddy happens to be one
of the richest landowners in the region. Sappy and corny, without
question, but Zane Grey does make us taste the dust of unwa-
tered ground and feel the heat of the naked desert sun. At a time

and in a place where "wheat is the most important thing in the world," as Grey wrote, weather matters. Weather, with its whims and wildness and fathomless power, is perhaps the most complex, fully developed character in *The Desert of Wheat*.

A more generous, but still powerfully hot and dry, weather suffuses Allis McKay's 1941 novel *They Came to a River*. A native of Washington's apple-growing country east of the Cascades, McKay made a name for herself with her first novel by following the golden rule of aspiring fiction writers: she wrote what she knew. *They Came to a River* is a big, sprawling, 650-page book about the lives and loves of the first families who planted irrigated orchards on the dry hillsides of the Columbia River in the early twentieth century. Weather, of course, looms large in any agricultural fiction—and McKay added the interesting twist of viewing weather from the perspective of apples. What's good for the apple harvest is good weather; whatever damages the fruit is bad weather. It's certainly a different way of looking at the atmosphere.

There are some meteorological surprises in store for the nonagricultural reader of *They Came to a River*. Spring, though it comes as a relief after the drab cold winter, is a season of worry, nervous anticipation, and fretful reckoning: "The buds were breaking now," McKay wrote of a lovely day in May. "Tom and Nate [two orchard owners] went anxiously from tree to tree, examining, counting, trying to estimate with still inexperienced eyes how many boxes of apples each tree would bear. The white blossoms broke out in a rash the second week of May. This time they were no random blooms, but a heavy white blanket that rolled clear from the river to the foot of the hill. The bees woke from their sleep and came down and thrummed busily in the thin sunshine."

As spring melts into summer, the sunshine intensifies and drought sets in. One might have assumed that farmers in this arid region would be praying for rain, but in fact, far from being a blessing, summer rain is one more potential plague: "This was the second summer in a row without any serious catastrophes to the crop; no pump trouble, no new diseases, no sultry 'moth weather,' no unwelcome rains. 'I should think you'd want the rain,' [Nate's wife] Chris had once said; 'it takes just that much load off the irrigating.' But Nate shook his head. 'It washes the spray from the fruit,' he said, 'and then we have to put it back on again.'" Rain brings more work and trouble than it's worth.

McKay was especially good at conjuring up the blast and heft of eastern Washington's fabled heat—but here too there are peculiarities unique to apple growing. Summer's dry heat is a blessing—as long as it doesn't stay too hot for too long. An elemental drama gets going late one summer as Nate and Chris eye their lovely swelling crop and worry about whether the hot weather will break in time for the apples to "color up." Nate informs his wife, "It must turn cool soon; and just at the right week—not too early, not too late—autumn must crack down sharply, sending spurs of red to flame across every tree. A man could do his best, tending and watering, thinning and spraying; but if the weather didn't turn at the right time all was lost."

And so we watch and wait with the apple growers for the season to turn. And we rejoice with them as the temperatures sink down magically, blessedly, right on schedule: "The days shortened, and the sunshine lost its rapier edge of heat. The nights were good and nippy now, and every morning Nate came in from an elated tour of the orchard to say that the color was beginning to come, the fruit was shaping up full and good." And then, as the brisk new season advances, the frenzied carnival of harvest commences—first the Jonathans and Spitzenburgs, then the Delicious, and finally, two weeks before Thanksgiving, the last of the dark red Winesaps, "the backbone of the crop."

Between them, Zane Grey and Allis McKay convey a bright, sharp impression of the *anxiety* that weather arouses in those who depend on the earth and the elements for their livelihoods. In a land of too little rain and unpredictable climatic extremes, the atmosphere can easily become an obsession: consciousness revolves around watching the sky, tuning in to the weather report, checking the thermometer and barometer, waiting and hoping and praying for rain, and cursing the sky when the rain fails to come or arrives too early or too late. This is not the leaden, unrelenting nightmare of the wet side, where, as H. L. Davis wrote, "the rain never totally stopped and the light never entirely started"—but it's just as crazy-making. In the agricultural fictions set east of the Cascades, weather is a kind of fickle, violent, unappeasable god—a god who never fails to remind humans of their weakness. How strange that the sun god of the Palouse, the Columbia River valley, and the Oregon high desert should have a blacker heart than the sullen overcast deity of the coast.

They Came to a River, largely forgotten today, is not a great work of art, but it's a good read, fresh and crisp as a new apple, and certainly as good as most of what makes it onto today's best-seller lists. Marriages, passionate dreams, births, deaths, family feuds, and love affairs keep the plot bubbling along—but what makes the book memorable is a kind of epic grandeur of men and women attempting something new on the land and succeeding at it richly. The accuracy and vividness with which McKay writes about apple-growing weather is typical of the book as a whole. She paints on a large but not pompous canvas, placing her characters in a harshly beautiful landscape that changes radically, sometimes violently, season by season. After reading *They Came to a River,* you'll stop and think about the next apple you eat—and you'll marvel for a moment at the dirt and work, and weather, that went into its creation.

A gap far more significant than time separates Allis McKay's 1941 *They Came to a River* from the American fictions written after World War II. Norman Mailer, Robert Lowell, Allen Ginsberg, Wallace Stegner, and Truman Capote, among other first-rate writers, launched their careers writing about a country torn up during the war years and sewn back afterward on an altogether different pattern.

Here in the Northwest, the aftermath of the war marked a literary coming of age. Our writers had finally put the pioneering days behind them. The region, if still rough and remote, was no longer new. Massive forest fires and clear-cuts had altered the landscape. Cities and their attendant sprawl of suburbs and industry were beginning to encroach on farmland and climb up wooded hillsides. Several generations of farmers and ranchers had tried, and often failed, to earn a living off the land. In postwar fictions and poems set in the Northwest, writers stepped back to take stock of what had happened to the region and its people. Irony and skepticism replaced wonder. Humor, disillusionment, outrage, reverence, and weariness became the dominant notes. Northwest writers, both homegrown and transplanted, were

shrewdly sizing up the elements that were special about and
peculiar to the region. Enormous wet forests. The ubiquity and
variety of water—salt, fresh, clear, frozen, flowing, rolling, snowing. The proximity of mountains. And of course the celebrated,
notorious, inescapable, interminable rain.

Bad weather became at once a joke and a badge of honor in
postwar Northwest literature. *Our weather is horrendous, but we love
it anyway* was one common stance. Or: *We endure it because it nourishes us*. Or: *We soak it in until it saturates us and then we go stark
raving mad*. Or *stark raving inspired*. "The primal source of poems:
wind, sea / and rain," native Seattle poet Richard Hugo proclaimed in his "Letter to Kizer from Seattle." Our weather was
becoming a literary motif in its own right, rather like the immigrant experience in New York, art and love in Paris, cinematic
glamour and betrayal in Los Angeles. In Northwest imaginative
writing after the war, weather started taking on a life of its own.

It was a life that kept cropping up in strange ways and unexpected places—never stranger than with the Beats, who stormed
through these parts in the 1950s and early 1960s and did their
own wild-eyed weather riffs. Although San Francisco and New
York were the Beat centers of gravity, the Pacific Northwest was
an important outpost—just an all-night hitchhike up the coast
from Berkeley. The region was also home turf to a member of the
Beat elite—poet Gary Snyder. Snyder hailed from Oregon, got
his undergraduate degree from Reed College, and afterward took
off periodically from his graduate studies to hole up in the Washington Cascades, where he chain-sawed timber and surveyed
mountain flanks from lookout towers during fire season. It was
Snyder who initiated novelist Jack (*On the Road*) Kerouac into the

damp mysteries of the region, even talking him into doing a stint as a fire lookout way up on the sacred fastness of Desolation Peak in the North Cascades. Although Kerouac supposedly went bug-eyed with boredom, he used the experience as the climax of his 1958 novel *The Dharma Bums*. In the book, the Snyder character, renamed Japhy Ryder, gets the writer-drinker-narrator Ray all fired up about the wonders of Desolation Peak while the two of them are swigging jug burgundy in a Marin County shack: "Desolation's way up there, Ray," Japhy tells him, "six thousand feet or so up looking into Canada and the Chelan highlands, the wilds of the Pickett range, and mountains like Challenger, Terror, Fury, Despair and the name of your own ridge is Starvation Ridge. . . . It'll be great for you Ray."

So Ray, after a marathon days-long party, hitchhikes north to Seattle, which greets him, naturally, with "a cold drizzle." Standing in his sweater and rain jacket on the deck of the Bremerton ferry, polishing off a half-pint of vodka, Ray surveys the scene and pronounces it "wet, immense, timbered, mountainous, cold, exhilarating, challenging."

Even wetter, colder, more challenging days descend once Ray gets into the mountains. Ray and the cussing mule driver Happy make the trek up to Desolation lookout during a summer storm of truly biblical awfulness—"heavy foggy rain" giving way to heavy sleety snow and blowing mists. Happy departs, leaving Ray alone and truly desolate on top of Desolation Peak: "It was the real Northwest grim and bitter misery."

But bliss is just over the horizon. When the storm finally blows out and the blue mountain scenery emerges from its cloud shroud, Ray attains a kind of instantaneous meteorological nirvana, an ecstatic cleansing and enlightenment through weather that leaves him wide-eyed with love and wonder. In his sixty days of alpine solitude, Ray gives himself up entirely to the cosmic pageant of mountain weather (there's actually little else to do, since no forest fires burn in his vicinity that summer): "My first sunset came and it was unbelievable. The mountains were covered with pink snow; the clouds were distant and frilly, like ancient remote cities of Buddhaland splendor; the wind worked incessantly, whish, whish, booming at times, rattling my ship. The new moon disk was prognathic and secretly funny in the pale plank of blue over the monstrous shoulders of haze that rose from Ross Lake. . . . Somewhere, it seemed, a golden festival of rejoicement was taking place." The weather stuns him with its variability; after the ferocious snowstorm of his arrival, a heat wave settles in: "There were days that were hot and miserable with locusts of plagues of insects, winged ants, heat, no air, no clouds, I couldn't understand how the top of a mountain in the North could be so hot." But the heat dissipates after a while with "wild lyrical drizzling rain, from the south, in the wind. . . ." Summer, Ray learns, is fleeting at 6,000 feet. August arrives "with a blast that shook my house and augured little augusticity" and before long, snow returns—"in a whirling shroud from Hozomeen by Canada, it came surling my way sending radiant white heralds through which I saw the angel of light peep . . . it was just too crazy."

And so, as autumn rolls in with "wild windy cloud-crazed days" and "all night gales of soaking rain," Ray prepares to make the descent back down to "this world." "Sixty sunsets had I seen revolve on that perpendicular hill," he chants in tranced Whitmanesque cadence. "The vision of the freedom of eternity was mine forever." Wow. Chalk one up for the transforming power of Northwest weather at its most sublime.

Ken Kesey, a kind of spiritual heir to the Beats, initially became famous as one of the Merry Pranksters, that wild and crazy band of druggy characters (including Beat hero Neal Cassady) who set 1960s counterculture spinning aboard their magic school bus (for details, read Tom Wolfe's *The Electric Kool-Aid Acid Test* and *Kesey's Garage Sale,* by Kesey himself). But Kesey, despite his youthful hallucinatory escapades, was not really a merry prankster at heart. He'd spent too many winters under western Oregon's gray skies for that—though born in Colorado, he grew up in Oregon and graduated from the University of Oregon in 1956. Eventually, after some adventures in California (where he studied writing at Stanford with Wallace Stegner, among others) and elsewhere, he returned to Oregon to settle in a town with the unKeseyesque name of Pleasant Hill. Kesey's Oregon—at least the Oregon he put into his big, meaty second novel, *Sometimes a Great Notion*—is not a place of Zen transfiguration or dreamy stoned hilarity: it's a wet, rough, hard-bitten, knobby, muddy slope of land stuck between mountain and ocean, where man and the elements wage ceaseless, hopeless war on each other. Man's role, embodied in the Stamper family, is to hack, saw, slash, and chop down whatever grows out of the earth, especially the big trees; nature's role is to dump down torrents of rain, saturate the earth, flood the rivers, erode the real estate, and infect man with mildew, skin rash, and fever blister. In the perpetual November of the soul that Kesey conjures up, only the tough survive: the untough "take that one-way dip" of suicide.

Sometimes a Great Notion, one of the great Northwest sagas, with a story crossing generations and encompassing the moral, social, political, and spiritual history of the state, contains some of the most graphically depressing evocations of winter wet ever set in type. Kesey pulls out all the stops as he recounts how the November rains got the folks of the grim coastal logging town of Wakonda to muttering and swearing and blaming everything rotten in their rotten lives on the rain:

> Because nothing can be done about the rain except
> blaming. And if nothing can be done about it, why
> get yourself in a sweat about it? Matter of fact, it can
> be convenient to have around. Got troubles with the
> old lady? It's the rain. Got worries and frets about the
> way the old bus is falling to pieces right under you?
> It's the ruttin' rain. Got a deep, hollow ache bleeding
> cold down inside the secret heart of you from too
> many deals fallen through? too many nights in bed
> with the little woman without being able to get it up?
> too much bitter and not enough sweet? Yeah? That
> there, brother, is just as well blamed on the rain; falls
> on the just and unjust alike, falls all day long all winter
> long every winter every year, and you might just as
> well give up and admit that's the way it's gonna be,
> and go take a little snooze. Or you'll be mouthin' the
> barrel of your twelve-gauge the way Evert Petersen at
> Mapleton did last year, or samplin' snail-killer the way
> both the Meriwold boys did over to Sweet Home. Roll
> with the blow, that's the easy out, blame it on the rain
> and bend with the wind, and lean back and catch

yourself forty winks—you can sleep real sound when
the rain is lullabying you. . . .

This is foul weather rising to the level of myth. This is weather
that might have tested Job or challenged Hercules. Weather as
cosmic adversary. Weather as plague. Weather as the embodi-
ment of everything in nature that means to thwart and mock and
madden human beings. Weather so all-encompassingly awful that
nothing outdoors matters *but* weather. This early November rain
pretty much keeps up for the duration of the novel—"dirty
motherin' rain," one character calls it; it's a rain that swells rivers,
rots flesh, drowns men, fills brains with an impenetrable fog, and
saturates the complex, twisted relations between the Stamper
brothers, wives, and patriarch. What Kesey lacks in strict meteorological accuracy, he more than makes up for in torrential
rushing narrative drive. In his novel, rain becomes a symbol for
the demonic spirit of the Northwest. H. L. Davis and Betty Mac-
Donald and plenty of others get us wet, but for Kesey the rain
isn't just weather—it's the fundamental condition of living and
dying in this part of the world.

Poet Richard Hugo also gets a lot of metaphorical mileage out of
the Northwest's foul weather. Hugo shares with Kesey a blue-
collar perspective, a taste for the grim, and a squinty-eyed
respect for what nature dishes out. Not a whole lot of sun shines
on their pages. Gray and wet are facts of life and, as far as they're
concerned, you'd better get used to it or get the hell out. Both
Kesey and Hugo are acutely attuned to how climate warps the
human spirit—only Hugo is less cosmic about it than Kesey. The
work of the poet, who died in 1982, is at once more realistic and

more internal than that of the novelist: Hugo's verse ripples with the actual slap and sting of Northwest rain and wind—but at some level of meaning, outer weather fuses with his own inner weather. Nobody does November better than Hugo.

Born in 1923, Hugo grew up in a rough working-class neighborhood with the celestial name of White Center, on the gritty margins of Seattle. The landscape that imprinted itself on Hugo's consciousness was not the dancing water of Puget Sound or the snow cone of Mount Rainier but rather the polluted backwaters of the "oily slow" Duwamish River and the immigrant shacks and "unswept taverns" of West Marginal Way. Though Hugo eventually escaped White Center, fleeing first to the University of Washington, where he studied poetry with Theodore Roethke in the late 1940s, and eventually to the University of Montana at Missoula, where he helped begin the writing program, much of his verse reflects the city's perpetually leaden sky—"the usual gray sky of Seattle turning the river gray," as he put it. The only time the sky grows calm and clear and luminous in Hugo's verse is when he is fishing.

Lashing rain, fog, and black gleaming puddles dampen the poems of Hugo's well-known 1961 collection *A Run of Jacks.* In "A Map of the Peninsula," he warns the artist who would paint the Olympic Peninsula that "fog that fakes the ocean's / outer rim will smear your canvas." "What is harsh" about this rain-soaked landscape, he explains, "is the bone-infecting / sound-deranging, forest-brooding damp." In the poem called "Duwamish," Hugo conjures up the essence of Seattle's "grim city winter" chill:

> Not silver cold
> like ice, for ice has glitter. Gray

cold like the river. Cold like 4 P.M.
on Sunday. Cold like a decaying porgy.

An insidious windstorm blows through the central stanza of
"Triangle for Green Men": starting with "slight warnings, / the
first movement of low grass," the storm mounts in height and
power until it blunts mountains, caves a fawn's ribs, and turns
rivers "on their sides in shock."

Memorable and invariably harsh weather images crop up in
later collections. In "Graves at Coupeville," a poem in the 1965
volume *Death of the Kapowsin Tavern,* Hugo's weather acquires a
voice, an angry one, and emotions, ugly ones. "When weather
shouted at us: vagabond," the poem begins. Weather eats away at
the words on the gravestones and chastens the poem's speaker
and his companions, who are reading and joking about the
inscriptions. "The weather hates our poses," the poem concludes,
"but the sun deranges men with laughter." "Cruelty and rain could
be expected. / Any season," he writes in the seething "The House
on 15th S.W." about his gray, violent childhood home. Cruelty
and rain: these are the conditions life has dealt him. Escape is a
fantasy of softer weather, "going north with clouds."

Hugo also puts some weather—plain and unretouched—into
the poems collected in the later volume *31 Letters and 13 Dreams*
(1977). In the letter-poems, most of them addressed to poet
friends, Hugo takes snapshots of what is happening around him,
be it a frozen fishing trip on Montana's Rainbow Lake or the dis-
orienting "dull placidity" of Miami or the welcoming warmth of a
beautiful bar in Milltown "where I pissed five years away / but
pleasantly." Whenever Hugo finds himself back in the Northwest,
weather seems to take center stage. Rain falls in "Letter to Kizer

from Seattle," of course, and he prays for even more rain, "one /
of those grim dark rolling southwest downpours" that he hopes
will persuade the city's electorate to vote to save Pike Place
Market. Rain comes down ceaselessly in "Letter to Wagoner from
Port Townsend," enough rain to make his very soul swim up to
the surface:

> Rain five days and I love it. . . .
> the grass explodes and trees
> rage black green deep as the distance they rage in. I
>   suppose
> all said, this is my soul, the salmon rolling in the strait
> and salt air loaded with cream for our breathing.

Weather is rarely the immediate subject of Hugo's poems, but
the moody damp and "wanton rain" of the Pacific Northwest seep
into his verse like dark water into an underground spring. There
is something blunt, threatening, implacable about Hugo's
weather: his is not the climate of hope nor of despair but of an
irreducible, starkly strange reality. The "wind is treason" in the
stormy July sea poem "Point No Point." "One cloud covers the
world pole to pole" in "How to Use a Storm," a poem in which
the weather is so bad that "moments are slower than days." He
recalls walking as a child beneath "catcalling clouds" in the poem
"White Center." "Why track down unity when the diffuse is so
exacting," he demands in the Roethke-influenced lyric "Keen to
Leaky Flowers":

> The world should always pour on us
> like this: chaos showering,
> each thing alone, dependent as a dream.

Here weather leapfrogs over metaphor into the realm of the metaphysical—not rain showering down but chaos itself, the diffuse, unknowable first principle of every Pacific storm. Hugo knows Northwest weather in his very bones.

Sometimes it takes a newcomer or an outsider to see ordinary phenomena like the vagaries of weather as they really are. Where a native son or longtime resident like H. L. Davis or Ken Kesey will exaggerate wildly, an outsider observing the seasonal round for the first time may record the facts with scrupulous precision. Bernard Malamud, a Jewish writer born in Brooklyn, New York, was the outsider par excellence when he moved to Corvallis, Oregon, in 1949 to take a position teaching writing at Oregon State College (now Oregon State University). Malamud stayed put in the Pacific Northwest for twelve years, launching his career as a novelist with *The Natural* (1952), *The Assistant* (1957), and *The Magic Barrel* (1958). And then, just weeks after he left Corvallis in 1961, he let fly with *A New Life,* a novel based on his years at OSC. *A New Life* is very much the outsider's novel: Malamud's hero Sy Levin, "formerly a drunkard" from the urban East, arrives at "Cascadia College" full of hope and high ideals about the liberal arts and vague dreamy notions about starting all over again in the expansive West. "What satirical wind blew you hither?" a colleague demands of the bearded, lonely Levin early on. "I came for the change you might say." "It's more than change," the colleague fires back, "it's transmogrification."

Levin's transmogrification is, for the most part, a plunge into deep disillusionment: the college turns out to be a snake pit of academic backbiting and narrow-minded turf-protection; his colleagues are viciously hostile to his desire to introduce a liberal arts curriculum; the "Cascadians" are chilly, self-satisfied, golf-playing suburbanites who conduct their lives behind drawn blinds; the students care far more about landing a good job after college than learning anything in class; the women Levin tries to seduce are aloof, deformed, bitter, and unforgiving. He does finally succeed in kindling a passionate love affair, but even that is fraught with seething issues and dark, adulterous complications. The new life dangles from the old life by a frayed, twisted cord.

Weather is omnipresent in *A New Life,* whistling through the narrative like an insistent leitmotif. From the moment of his arrival, Levin scrutinizes the region's atmospheric changes with a careful, consuming interest—the interest of the newcomer. Since he's alone so much, especially in the first few months, and since he doesn't own a car, weather *matters* a lot to Levin. He's acutely sensitive to seasonal shifts, to the dire warnings of winter gloom issued by natives, to the contrast between East Coast and Pacific Northwest weather patterns. In fact, weather becomes a kind of barometer for the transmogrification Levin endures in the course of the academic year. Arriving at the end of August, when the weather is "practically flawless," Levin revels in the "open sky," dark evergreens, and glowing flowers. But a faculty wife promptly sets him straight about the looming damp reality. "It rains here?" Levin asks her in mild disbelief on a glorious late summer day.

"It does. It almost drove me mad at first but I've learned to live with it. The trick is no longer to love the sun. . . . It rains, for instance, most of the fall and winter and much of the spring. It's a spongy sky you'll be wearing on your head. . . . Many Cascadians want rain and warmth rather than sunlight and cold." Levin, "a city boy let loose," takes to watching the skies for signs of sponginess. Summer at first seems reluctant to depart: "For weeks the blue sky was cloudless but lately huge white masses drifted in from the Pacific." When the autumn rains do arrive, Levin marvels at the shimmering, mercurial, iridescent quality of the atmosphere:

> Usually the morning was overcast between wettings,
> the moving sky continuously surprising. Overhead
> the clouds roiled dark; ahead thinning through shades
> of gray to an accident of gold. To the north above
> the dark green hills, a moody blue. In the west white
> steam shrouded the mountain tops. Depending on the
> direction he looked, above could be gold, black, silver,
> gray. He had never in his life gazed so long at sky,
> probed so often the places of light, threads bursting,
> spoonfuls burning, webs of glowing caught in trees.
> Around noon, if it was going to, the sun poked its
> steaming eye through the mist, and clouds broke into
> rivers and lakes, creating blue afternoons. Marvelous.

But then, inevitably, winter wet descends in earnest, the marvelous shrivels and sinks, and Levin feels the black water of despair rising around him: "Levin walked in the cold rain, the wettest, dreariest he had ever been in. The town was tight around his shoulders, the wet streets long and dark, street lights obscure at corners. A man could drown mid-block and nobody would know. It was after eight but half the houses he passed were totally dark. On rainy nights people went to bed; it was, after all, a diversion for the married. . . ." But winter is just beginning. Levin's meteorological initiation won't be complete until rain falls in his very soul and his saturated spirit pours forth a spontaneous poetry of rain. The sea change comes on him soon after Christmas. Lying in bed, awake and restless in the middle of the night, Levin listens to the rain "as natural history, the Pacific extending itself over the land," and he thinks back over his past:

> In the dark Levin remembered the rain of his childhood, blown in wind against the faces of tenements, engulfing the leafless backyard tree in foaming bursts; but when it had ended—after a day, three, a week— it had ended and enter light, the worshipful sun. Here was no sense of being between rains; it was a climate, a condition, the water burbling, thick, thin, fine, ubiquitous, continuous, monotonous, formless. Once in a while he saw two rainbows in the same sky but after rainbows it rained. Wherever Levin went he went in rubbers, raincoat, umbrella. . . . Students stood bareheaded in the pelting rain, talking leisurely, even opening a book to prove a point. Meanwhile Levin had grown neither fins nor duckfeathers; nor armorplate against loneliness.

Lonely and wet, Levin hits bottom and finds himself mysteriously ascending back to the surface. True, the rain never stops, but the consolation is that cold weather, true Siberian blasting cold, never sets in. Levin receives his reprieve from snow and ice with guilty pleasure—"as though he had helped murder [winter], or got something for nothing when they read the will." Gradually, he opens his eyes to the small, shining fruits of mildness—the winter primroses that he had failed to notice in bloom, the slick green daffodil stems already two inches high at Christmas, the

January crocuses. "On New Year's day naked jasmine in the back-yard by the cherry tree touched the dark world with its yellow light; forsythia performed the same feat a few weeks later. Camellias were budding in January; quince and heather in flower, petals touching the stillest air." How many Northeastern or Mid-western transplants have experienced the same flush of surprise at the year-round flow of sap in the Pacific Northwest—the flowers in winter, the spring buds swelling even before the autumn leaves are quite gone, grass and weeds growing vigor-ously under the sparse wet winter snows?

And so Levin, wetter but wiser, survives his baptism in North-west weather. Malamud's primary agenda in *A New Life* may have been to satirize (and scandalize) the English department at Oregon State College, but in putting Levin through the weary paces of an academic year, he also found a brilliant way of sum-moning up the pageant of seasons in western Oregon. Levin's meteorological appraisal is fresh, wide-eyed, funny, incredu-lous—the exact sequence of stunned reactions that newcomers cycle through in the course of their first year here and that natives always laugh at them for. *A New Life* remains one of the most sen-sitive and accurate weather portraits in our literature.

It was bound to happen. After a century and more of writers wailing and wallowing, documenting and dreading, conjuring and cursing the rain, somebody had to come along and hymn its praises. Not just appreciate the rain, but fall down on damp knees and throw streaming hands heavenward and revel in its soaking splendor. Enter David James Duncan, unknown Oregon writer and fishing fanatic, who appeared out of the blue in 1983 with *The River Why,* a brilliant, freewheeling, loose-jointed, crack-pated paean to fly-fishing the wondrous rivers of western Oregon. Gus Hale-Orviston, the book's young hero and narrator, is a self-proclaimed "fishing genius" who holes up in a cabin on a swift-flowing river near the Oregon coast and embarks on a kind of mystical orgy of fly-casting. At the climax of the book, Gus, who has been fasting and praying and abstaining from fishing for days, experiences a kind of spiritual catharsis—a cleansing of wounds, a consuming of cares, an enlightenment of mind—all precipitated by the sweet arrival of the autumn rains. It's a gorgeously sodden moment in the literature of Northwest weather:

> For three days it rained, almost without sound,
> almost without ceasing. It was the first good rain since
> the August showers . . . a rain that hummed on the
> river pool and pattered on new puddles, washing
> the songbirds south, bringing newcomers from the
> north—rain birds, water lovers. . . . It was a rain that
> plucked the last leaves from the trees, turned stone
> gullies into streams, set the water ouzels singing. . . .
> Yet while the rain fell I didn't fish—only watched and
> rested, and I was lulled and cradled, caressed and
> enveloped in a cool, mothering touch that washed
> away the wounds of the summer; and my old, unmiti-
> gated longings—even the longings for fish, for Eddy,
> for the Friend—were changed from gnawing, aching
> dissatisfactions into a kind of sad, silent music, and the
> hollow place those longings had carved in me became
> a kind of sanctuary, an emptiness I grew used to, grew

satisfied to leave unfilled. Reckoning up these transfor-
mations, watching the rain that began the day I sat
at the source, I realized that I *had* been given a spirit-
helper: I had been given this rain.

Blessed with this precious wet gift from heaven, Gus emerges
from his hermitlike solitude, finally connects with Eddy (the girl
of his dreams), romances and marries her, experiences the
delights of a fishing honeymoon, and somewhere along the way
receives a glowing vision of the Great Fisherman in the sky—"the
light and the hook were his . . . and were made of love alone." A
flood of happily-ever-after joy is released by a three-day Oregon
soaker. A quirky, funny, original book, a hybrid of novel, memoir,
fishing tale, spiritual quest, fantasy, and coming-of-age narrative,
The River Why gave a new twist to the old story of Northwest rain.
Rain as healer. Rain as spirit-helper. Rain as transformer of land
and river, animals and people. Others had seen the beauty of our
rains, but Duncan revealed their *meaning*. And he did it not only
with grace but with humor. Let it pour.

Duncan did it beautifully, but he did not do it first. Rainiac
Tom Robbins also worshiped rain in print—in fact, he may have
founded the cult. Several large puddles separate Duncan and
Robbins stylistically. If Duncan opens the door and welcomes in
the rain, Tom Robbins unscrews the doors from their jambs and
runs outside naked. A native of North Carolina, Robbins arrived
in Seattle in the early 1960s, worked as an editor and reviewer for
various Seattle newspapers, covered (and evidently participated
in) the local psychedelic scene, hung out with artists and hippies,
in 1970 relocated to La Conner, Washington, and in 1971 published his first novel, *Another Roadside Attraction*. It is the quintes-

sential 1960s improvisation—loopy, fragmented, surreal, wildly funny, totally irreverent (the plot revolves around a Skagit Valley hot dog stand that has somehow become the new resting place for the body of Christ), free-associative to the brink of psychosis, and ultimately upbeat (here it parts company with the mood of the late '60s). Robbins tosses into the book everything he had ever seen, felt, thought, or imagined, along with some fabulous, highly wrought (overwrought?), all but Homeric evocations of Northwest rain, as here at the commencement of the rainy season in Skagit Valley:

> And then the rains came.
> They came down from the hills and up from the Sound.
> And it rained a sickness. And it rained a fear. And it rained an odor. And it rained a murder. And it rained dangers and pale eggs of the beast.
> Rain fell on the towns and the fields. It fell on the tractor sheds and the labyrinth of sloughs. Rain fell on toadstools and ferns and bridges. It fell on the head of John Paul Ziller.
> Rain poured for days, unceasing. Flooding occurred. The wells filled with reptiles. The basements filled with fossils. Mossy-haired lunatics roamed the dripping peninsulas. Moisture gleamed on the beak of the Raven. Ancient shamans, rained from their homes in the dead tree trunks, clacked their clamshell teeth in the drowned doorways of forests. Rain hissed on the Freeway. It hissed at the prows of fishing boats. It ate the old warpaths, spilled the huckleberries, ran in the ditches. Soaking. Spreading. Penetrating.

And it rained an omen. And it rained a poison. And
it rained a pigment. And it rained a seizure.

And so on. A few hundred pages later, after a "peekaboo
summer," the rains are back, falling harder, faster, with a fiercer
rhetorical frenzy than ever:

It fell in sweeps and it fell in drones. It fell in
unending cascades of cheap Zen jewelry. It fell on the
dikes. It fell on the firs. It fell on the downcast necks
of the mallards.
And it rained a fever. And it rained a silence. And it
rained a sacrifice. And it rained a miracle. And it
rained sorceries and saturnine eyes of the totem.
Rain drenched the chilly green tidelands. The river
swelled. The sloughs fermented. Vapors rose from
black stumps on the hillsides. Spirit canoes paddled in
the mists of the islands. Legends were washed from
desecrated burial grounds. . . .
And it rained a screaming. And it rained a rawness.
And it rained a plasma. And it rained a disorder.

This is pretty heady stuff. But Robbins had by no means
written himself dry on the subject. Two decades later, after
soaking up countless more Pacific storms, he let fly once again
with an exuberantly cracked meteorological hosanna in an essay
entitled "Why I Live in Northwestern Washington." "I'm here for
the weather," he begins with a sly chuckle, flying smack in the face
of expectation. After reeling off a few other things he's here for,
including volcanoes and geoducks and "the flying saucers that
made their first public appearance near Mount Rainier" and the
women "with their quaint Norwegian brand of lust," Robbins gets
down to the real business at hand, the awful weather he so dearly

loves: "A steady, wind-driven rain composes music for the psyche. It not only nurtures and renews, it consecrates and sanctifies. It whispers in secret languages about the primordial essence of things."

Even in the droughts of summer, Robbins does not despair, for he knows the rains will return sooner or later—sometimes much sooner than anyone imagines. "Our sky can go from lapis to tin in the blink of an eye," he declaims merrily. "Blink again and your latte's diluted. And that's just fine with me. I thrive here on the certainty that no matter how parched my glands, how anhydrous the creek beds, how withered the weeds in the lawn, it's only a matter of time before the rains come home." At this point, just as he seems to be limbering up for one of his swooping rhetorical swan dives, Robbins cheats a bit and dips back into the old well of *Another Roadside Attraction,* lifting with only minor alterations the passages about raining a fever and a sacrifice, a screaming and a rawness. A minor sin—and who could resist recycling such glorious poetry of rain? "Yes, I'm here for the weather," the essay concludes. "And when I'm lowered at last into a pit of marvelous mud, a pillow of fern and skunk cabbage beneath my skull, I want my epitaph to read, IT RAINED ON HIS PARADE. AND HE WAS GLAD!" Pure Robbins.

You'd never know, from the region's literary output, that the past couple of decades have been on the dry side in the Pacific Northwest (with a few notably torrential exceptions). Whatever the "real" weather, rain keeps falling steadily in the imaginations of contemporary poets, novelists, and essayists. If anything, the literary climate has grown wetter of late, nursing up an ever lusher diversity of responses. I'll close with one more pluvial celebration—a passage from Sallie Tisdale's 1991 volume *Stepping Westward* that furnishes an interesting counterpoint to Tom Robbins's damp effusions. Tisdale, the great-great-great-granddaughter of Oregon pioneers, creates a splendid hybrid in this book by crossbreeding memoir, regional history, travelogue, and ecological appreciation. Her method is to start from the personal and work outward, documenting her involvement with and reactions to Northwest landscapes, people, industries, myths, dreams—and, of course, weather, as in this account of an excursion out to the wet old town of Astoria near the mouth of the Columbia River (not far from Lewis and Clark's winter camp):

> A friend of mine calls these sleeting rains, where the drops are so heavy and pregnant they elongate as they fall, "celestial threads." There were shadows under each little, rolling wave. People hunched over in yellow slickers fished from every half-rotten pier or boulder, and they were catching. The lichen-coated trees get brighter in the rain, an aquarium sea-green fuzzy against the dark russet forest. The red bark and bush are warmer, the fields greener in the rain; it adds to the great endurance of the landscape for me. No vista is the same twice, because the sky is never the same twice here, the light never repeats. And there's no point in trying to stay dry. There's nowhere to walk, no place to stand. Mist clings to the hillsides like torn tissue, and when it has finally passed, a calm settles over the hills and trees—a satisfied, moistened calm. Ah, everything sighs. Aaah.

Calmer, sweeter, sadder, and saner than Robbins, Tisdale lifts her face heavenward not in ecstasy but in exultant acceptance— the acceptance of someone who has lived under a wet sky most of her life, who has left it for hotter, drier, easier climes but has returned because she belongs here.

Rain belongs here too—more than people do, perhaps. Rain nourishes even as it rots. It creates and obscures. Colors and leaches out color. It falls harder in some seasons than others; it passes, freezes, blows over, dries up, but it always comes back. And it shows no sign of letting up, inside or out. Especially in our poems and stories, novels and memoirs and essays. "There's no point in trying to stay dry," Tisdale declares as the heavens open over Astoria. The same can be said of the old wet city of the imagination. Rain makes our literary endeavors rich and strange. It waters our creative powers. It is, in a sense, our most precious literary capital. Lucky for us, as the decades roll on, our writers keep splashing their riches around with ever increasing ingenuity, generosity, and joyous abandon.

Spring

As far as I can tell, spring in the Northwest is our payback for autumn. What we miss of New England crisp and crunch in October, we make up for with the slow sumptuous parade of spring flowers—a parade that commences well before the official beginning of the season and goes on, seemingly, forever. Connoisseurs of spring flowers can, if they're so inclined, experience a kind of perpetual spring in the region—beginning with the February daffodils of southern Oregon and culminating with the wild flowers that bloom on the alpine meadows of Mount Rainier in early August. Unlike New England, which often experiences a sudden, violent transition from winter to summer—a zillion cherry trees may burst into blossom in an April heat wave and get stripped bare two days later in a thunderstorm—the Northwest has a spring of gentle, halting transitions prompted by fitful, undecided weather patterns.

It's a blurry season, a season without clear boundaries. When I lived back East, there always came a soft fragrant morning when I would poke my nose out the door, sniff, and murmur blithely to anyone who would listen, "Ah, spring is in the air." But that doesn't seem to happen here—or it happens so many times that it ceases to mean anything. The green creeps up on you so gradually and so ceaselessly that you hardly notice when early spring's "grave green dust" (as poet Elizabeth Bishop has it) deepens and unfolds into juicy leaves. Some days the green wears a mantle of leaking gray. Other times it almost vibrates in the strong white light. Pouring showers clear out while your back is turned.

Rainbows become as commonplace as primroses. In spring,
the atmosphere can cycle through a full round of seasons in
a single day—from frosty winter morning to summery noon
to autumnal twilight. Spring weather advances and retreats
erratically, chaotically, with no apparent rhyme or reason.
"We are having about two-thirds of the time the most delightful weather imaginable," Seattle pioneer Catharine P. Blaine
wrote the folks back home in the spring of 1854. "The rest
of the time it is as gloomy and dreary as rain and cloudy
skies can make it." Late March can bring days twenty degrees
warmer than mid-May. Clouds pour in from the south when
you thought you were done with them. April is a toss-up
from year to year, week to week. And then, as the days
lengthen gloriously and the earth warms and the lakes and
sounds beckon, comes the heartbreak of June. June the gray,
the cool, the reluctant.

So far, every Northwest spring has taken me by surprise.
Just when I think I have the weather figured, it changes. Take
1996—a spring when even the most ardent rain-lover was
hoping for a break. As the season commenced, it looked as if
the torrents of winter were over, and I exulted in my journal
on March 19:

> Like a giant sponge wrung of its last few drops of
> water or a leaky faucet wrenched shut, the sky has
> ceased to pour out water on the land and now instead
> sends sprinkles—or nothing. Clouds roll in, thicken,
> darken—ominously—and then break up. The forecast
> calls for scattered showers, few showers, occasional
> showers, chance of showers, isolated showers—but
> only a freckling of rain actually darkens the pave-
> ments. Then the sun breaks through, then a cloud

blows over—but not enough rain falls to dampen a
mop. The rain has ended—the real rain.

What did I know? Turns out this was only a brief dry spell. By
April 23, spring was looking distinctly less sparkly:

> Rainy season over? Not exactly. Yes, we had some sun
> on Saturday, April 20, and Sunday was quite a lovely
> day, warm and mostly clear, maybe mid-60s, with a
> slight haze and milky clouds to the south. But Monday,
> yesterday, dawned damp and drizzly and it rained
> lightly most of the day, pausing for gray grim cloudy
> sun glare in late afternoon, then starting up again in
> earnest last night. And it has been raining steadily,
> sometimes harder sometimes softer but always coming
> down, ever since. Rained all night. Gives every indica-
> tion of raining all day. I'd say we'll get 2-plus inches by
> the time it's over—already gotten 1.5, I think. A real
> spring soaker, highs in the low to mid-50s. The wind
> is supposed to kick up and blow hard this afternoon
> and this evening. Then they're saying it will clear out
> by the weekend. Looks like April will be above
> average in precip, as were October, November,
> December, January, and February. Only March slightly
> below. Wet. Weeds everywhere.

And the wet went right on:

> April 30: Yes and I mean wet. It rained all day Tuesday
> with a brief break in the late afternoon. It was okay
> for some of Wednesday, then some downpours late in
> the day. Thursday—light or moderate rain mostly all
> day, finally clearing off, sort of, by 4 P.M. or so.
> Friday—nice in the morning, then heavy downpours
> with hail in the afternoon. Clearing. More rain and

hail. Saturday nice. Sunday some sprinkles and gloomy.
Yesterday, Monday, nice. Today gloomy with thickening clouds. The forecast for upper 60s and low 70s
never materialized. Now they're saying cool, showery
weather will continue all weekend. Last week it rained
so much it drove my friends Joyce and Regis back to
New York City, three days before they had planned to
end their vacation. They just couldn't take it anymore.
Everyone here terribly amused by *that*. We *told* them
not to come until summer. . . . Total April rain at Sea-
Tac 5.5 inches—about double normal. But for once I
think we had more here. That old convergence zone.
Enough already. I'm freezing. And nothing will grow if
it doesn't warm up.

May 14: *Rainy season returns.* How awfully depressing.
The promised sunny spell never came, though it did
get warmer. Instead we had some sun breaks, as I
recall, but mostly gloom on Friday, followed by drizzling rain on Saturday morning, a glaring and warmish
afternoon. At some point I noticed a halo around the
sun—never a good sign. Sunday gave promise of finer
weather, though it felt heavy and humid; we hung
around in the mostly sunny but high overcast morning;
got some sprinkles in the afternoon, then a steadier
harder rain set up Sunday night and we had periods
of rain and mid-60s yesterday. It was raining steadily
when we got up this morning. Now, midmorning,
it's gray and overcast and heavy and leaden. I heard
someone say we were due for weeks and endless
weeks of this—something to do with a blocking high
in Alaska, giving them record warmth but directing
the jet stream south onto us. What a mess. It's the

endless depressing gray sog factor that is so hard to
take—a wet cool spring after a record wet rainy
season. We *really* need some sun. It is, after all, mid-
May. The slugs are unbelievable—huge and fat and
slimy. On the plus side, the moist air has this sweet
smell, and of course the grass is greener than green.
Tulips have stayed in bloom a solid month. But annuals
are not growing—too cool. Too wet.

To my chagrin, it rained nearly every day in May. Gardeners were driven to distraction. "The plants just sit in the
ground and *sulk*," a horticultural comrade of mine wailed.
Most conversations began, "Can you *believe* it's *still* raining?"
It would have been a joke if it weren't so depressing. And
if it hadn't been raining since the previous September. Yes,
"rains all the time" and all that, but this was unnatural.

Statistically, I had some justification for assuming the heavy
rains would cease at the start of spring, for Seattle's average
monthly precipitation drops from 3.54 inches in March to
2.33 in April and 1.7 in May; the statistics for Portland are
comparable: 3.6 in March, 2.4 in April, 2.1 in May. And as
precipitation falls off, average temperatures climb—from a
daily maximum of 52.7° in March to 57.2° in April, 63.9° in
May, and 69.9° in June in Seattle; Portland is even balmier,
with daily averages maxing out at 55.9° in March, 60.4° in
April, 67.1° in May, and 73.9° in June. Sounds pretty nice,
doesn't it? The trouble is, means and normals seem to signify
even less in spring than in other seasons. There have been
springs when temperatures limped along dismally in the 20s
and 30s—1952, for example, when the temperature at Sea-
Tac airport dropped to 29° on April 7 and 8, 33° on May 2,
and 38° on June 12. In April 1991, Sea-Tac measured 6.53
inches of rain—more than the norm for December; and a

staggering, record-breaking 8.4 inches of rain fell in March 1950 (it rained a total of 194 days that year, the most since records have been kept at Sea-Tac). Back before there was a Sea-Tac, in March 1879, Seattle received 11.92 inches of rain—proof that it really did rain more in the old days. On the other hand, temperatures in the 90s are not unknown in May, and the thermometer has hit the 80s in April a handful of times in the past few decades. In May 1963, Seattle went twenty-six days without rain, and five years earlier there were twenty-two rainless May days, seven days when temperatures climbed into the 80s, and twelve days in the 70s. Positively Hawaiian.

Conventional wisdom has it that May is nicer than June west of the mountains, and there is some basis for this in meteorological fact. According to Walter Rue in *Weather of the Pacific Coast,* the hot high sun of June causes a rapid warming in the arid region east of the Cascades—average daytime highs in Yakima, for example, jump from 71.6° in May to 79.9° in June. This jump in temperature creates "thermal lows" in eastern Washington and Oregon that pull in air from the west. The westward movement of air sets up an onshore flow, with moist marine air streaming in off the ocean and shrouding the Puget Sound basin in clouds. Hence the depressing gloomy spells that hit just at the threshold of summer.

T. S. Eliot wrote austerely of midwinter spring in England, an eerily bright suspended time when "the brief sun flames the ice, on pond and ditches . . ." Sallie Tisdale has written exuberantly of midspring summer in Oregon, "a week that comes every year" in March or April—"this one week when everything relaxes and the tension of winter slips from the twigs and dirt and the anxious infant leaves in a kind of ecstasy. Everything grows madly night and day, hurtling toward summer like a racehorse given its lead to run. This week, already, is the most wealthy week, a slightly drunken week, sexy and full of promise." Seattle's pioneering Methodist minister David Blaine experienced just such an intoxicating spell in early April 1854 (though I'm not sure he perceived it as drunken and sexy): "Last week and the week before we had the most beautiful weather, long, clear, mild days with hardly a cloud visible and with a sweet springlike atmosphere, so soothing and cheering that I thought, 'What a pleasant country this is for invalids.'"

Even in the horribly wet spring of 1996, though Mother Nature couldn't quite swing a balmy *week,* we did eke out a single day of sunny ecstasy—April 7 (as it happened, it was Easter Sunday), when the temperature hit a record-breaking 78° in Seattle and flowers burst out in unbelievable profusion. "It's too much sweetness coming all at once," I wrote in my weather journal, little realizing that I'd have to hoard this single day for the next three months (it didn't hit 80° that year until July 7, tying the record for the latest date). Spring in the Northwest is sure to bring showers, gloomy days, unseasonable chill—but it also bestows blessings of such weeks (or hours), for which all living things rejoice.

And then there is the curse of Northwest spring: flooding. In a typical year snow has been building up in the mountains since October, and it often goes on building well into spring. Paradise Ranger Station on Mount Rainier generally gets over 50 inches of snow in April. At some point most of that snow is going to melt, and when it does, floods are likely to occur. Two of the worst flood years in recorded history were 1894 and 1948, and both had similar weather conditions: cold wet winters, cool temperatures continuing into May, and then a

sudden warming that rapidly melted deep snowpacks. The
flood of 1894 commenced after heavy rain fell on the Columbia River drainage basin in late May. Portland and its environs
got hit very hard that spring: water covered a good deal of
the northern section of the city, rail service was suspended,
and people used boats to get around. Oregonians were even
treated to the unsettling spectacle of farm buildings drifting
down swollen rivers. At peak flow in June, 1,240,000 cubic
feet of water flowed past The Dalles *every second*.

The flood of 1948 did not quite match the volume of
1894: The Dalles saw only 1,010,000 cubic feet per second
of water roar past that June. But the 1948 flood took more
lives and destroyed far more property. Water levels on the
Columbia and its tributaries started rising in mid May and
crested by the end of the month. "Crest" is perhaps a mis-
leading word—for this flood was not like a single wave of
water but rather a plateau that soared up and stayed up for
weeks. Water remained above flood stage for forty-five consecutive days at Portland and fifty-one days at Vancouver,
Washington. At least fifty-one people died in the flood, and
crops growing on a quarter million acres were spoiled. The
disaster climaxed in a frozen moment of tragedy when a dike
alongside the Columbia near Vanport, Oregon, broke at 4:15
on the afternoon of May 30. As *Weatherwise* reported, "A wall
of water poured through the break with such rapidity that few
of the 18,700 residents escaped with little more than the
clothing they were wearing. Within an hour, the town was
completely destroyed and at least 16 persons lost their lives."
Walter Rue added: "The city, once America's largest war-time
housing project, was wiped out in less than an hour. Men and
women swam frantically for the dikes. Policemen and others
on dikes that remained standing threw ropes into the water

and people pulled themselves along, hand-over-hand to safety." The flood finished off Vanport for all time: the city was never rebuilt.

Spring floods have inspired some memorable passages in Northwest literature. My favorite literary flood is in Marilynne Robinson's haunting first novel *Housekeeping,* set in the rugged mountain and lake country of northern Idaho. Winter has ended in the town of Fingerbone with "three days of brilliant sunshine and four of balmy rain," and the snow has softened to leaky slush. The narrator, a lonely, brooding girl named Ruth, describes how the rising waters transform everything inside and out: "My grandmother always boasted that the floods never reached our house, but that spring, water poured over the thresholds and covered the floor to the depth of four inches, obliging us to wear boots while we did the cooking and washing up. We lived on the second floor for a number of days. . . . The woodpile was full of spiders and mice, and the pantry curtain rod was deeply bowed by the weight of water climbing the curtains. If we opened or closed a door, a wave swept through the house, and chairs tottered, and bottles and pots clinked and clunked in the bottoms of the kitchen cabinets."

Spring floods are becoming more common and more serious in the Northwest as clear-cuts proliferate, parking lots and malls pave over drainage areas, and new subdivisions sprout up in floodplains. Even without spreading development, the rivers that flow west from the Cascade and Olympic mountain crests are extremely prone to flooding: the terrain they traverse is relatively brief and often steep, and when winter snows melt, an awful lot of water flows down awfully hard and fast. As I write this, spring is exactly two weeks away and all the elements are in place for major flooding throughout the Northwest. Snowpack is unusually deep this year, approaching record levels in many areas, and just in the past week or so the mountains have picked up several more feet of snow. If the forecast is right, more snow will accumulate at least through next week. Someday, we earnestly hope and pray, the sun is going to come out again and stay out for a week or two. The mercury is going to climb into the 60s and 70s in the lowlands. And all that snow up there, twenty feet deep and more in places, is going to melt. If we're lucky, it will melt gradually, trickling down to the roots of ancient firs and hemlocks. If we're unlucky, it will melt under torrents of warm rain—flood weather. Either way, one thing is certain: the mud this year is going to be something else.

"Each day the light sprayed the sky like a hose," wrote Annie Dillard of May in Whatcom County (in the far northwest corner of Washington) in her big, densely peopled historical novel *The Living*. "It was indeed the month of May, and the light never quit. People grew fitful, bold, or melancholy." After the ceaseless winter rains, the assault of spring light proves to be too much for some of Dillard's characters: "On the first sunny day in May, Mr. Evan Vernon, a partner in the Whatcom Savings Bank, had shot himself in the earhole with a sawed-off shotgun. It happened every spring." And so it goes. Northwest spring is a quirky season, in fiction and in fact—a season of bliss and panic and unbearable relief. Dillard's Mr. Evan Vernon is an extreme case, but she's right that the limitless sunshine does strange things to people after the months of dark and wet. Here in the Northwest, spring fever is often a fever of dislocation. It doesn't quite seem real, all this sun and warmth and blinding light. It's jarring. It doesn't "fit" the landscape. We worry that it's all going to vanish. And maybe deep down, in some damp wintry cave of the heart, we wish it would.

I knew I was becoming acclimatized to the weather of the Northwest when I took a trip to Los Angeles at the end of my first spring. It had rained hard in Seattle the night before, and it was cool and misty the morning of our flight, with clouds massed around Mount Rainier—huge muscular archipelagos of clouds separated by little rivulets of blue sky. I could tell, even without listening to the forecast, that the clouds would break up and sail across the sky all day—an endless armada of white against blue. It was June 21, the day on which spring and summer embrace, the longest day of the year. A *very* long day in Seattle—with the sun rising at 5:12 A.M. (daylight saving time) and remaining above the horizon until 9:10 at night. But numbers fail to convey what happens after sundown—the lingering breathtaking reddish glimmer in the northern sky that sweeps the imagination up the Sound to Canada and Alaska and all the way to the blazing sky of the Arctic Circle, where sunrise follows on the heels of sunset in the endless day of the polar solstice.

Meanwhile, as my thoughts winged north, our plane was already banking over California: we had left the clouds behind somewhere in Oregon, the sky was a perfect hazy blue from ocean to Sierra, the green of the Northwest forest had given way to a parched brown. When we landed in Los Angeles at midday the temperature was nearing 80°, the sun was shining through a thin film of smog, a light breeze was blowing—and it stayed that way for the next four days of our visit, and the next forty days beyond, for all I know. The weather, as they always say, was perfect. But I kept thinking that it wasn't really *weather*.

Here in the Northwest, the weather, God knows, is rarely
perfect and often downright awful. But it's real weather,
"extravagant weather," as Marilynne Robinson called it, and
occasionally great weather, and it gives this region life and
character and something to write home about. "How can you
stand it?" they ask me when I go back East to visit. "Isn't it
awfully wet out there?" I used to protest, reel out compara-
tive rainfall statistics, brag about the mild winters, the long
flowery springs, the low humidity of summer, the cool
evenings. Now I just shrug, like a true Northwesterner. "You
get used to it," I say, and change the subject.

SELECT BIBLIOGRAPHY
Northwest History, Culture, Climate, and Geology

Bingham, Edwin R., and Glen A. Love, eds. *Northwest Perspectives: Essays on the Culture of the Pacific Northwest*. Eugene: University of Oregon Press, 1979.

Cantwell, Robert. *The Hidden Northwest*. Philadelphia: J. B. Lippincott Co., 1972.

Edwards, G. Thomas, and Carlos A. Schwantes, eds. *Experiences in a Promised Land: Essays in Pacific Northwest History*. Seattle: University of Washington Press, 1986.

Holbrook, Stewart H. *Burning an Empire: The Story of American Forest Fires*. New York: Macmillan, 1943.

Jackman, E. R., and R. A. Long. *The Oregon Desert*. Caldwell, Idaho: Caxton Printers, 1964.

Kruckeberg, Arthur R. *The Natural History of Puget Sound Country*. Seattle: University of Washington Press, 1991.

Lavender, David. *Land of Giants: The Drive to the Pacific Northwest, 1750–1950*. Garden City, N.Y.: Doubleday, 1958.

Meany, Edmond S. *History of the State of Washington*. New York: Macmillan, 1909.

Morgan, Murray. *The Last Wilderness*. New York: Viking Press, 1955.

Robbins, William G., Robert J. Frank, and Richard E. Ross, eds. *Regionalism and the Pacific Northwest*. Corvallis: Oregon State University Press, 1983.

Schwantes, Carlos A. *The Pacific Northwest: An Interpretive History*. Lincoln: University of Nebraska Press, 1989.

Scott, James W., and Roland L. De Lorme. *Historical Atlas of Washington*. Norman: University of Oklahoma Press, 1988.

The Age of Exploration

Allen, John Logan. *Passage Through the Garden: Lewis and Clark and the Image of the American Northwest*. Urbana: University of Illinois Press, 1975.

Ambrose, Stephen E. *Undaunted Courage: Meriwether Lewis, Thomas Jefferson, and the Opening of the American West*. New York: Simon & Schuster, 1996.

Cook, James. *A Voyage to the Pacific Ocean*. London: G. Nicol & T. Cadell, 1784.

Fletcher, Francis. *The World Encompassed by Sir Francis Drake*. London: Nicholas Bourne, 1628.

Lewis, Meriwether, and William Clark. *The Original Journals of the Lewis and Clark Expedition,* ed. Reuben Gold Thwaites. New York: Dodd, Mead, 1905.

Vancouver, George. *A Voyage of Discovery to the North Pacific Ocean and Round the World.* London: C. G. and J. Robinson, 1798.

Early Settlers, Pioneers, and Visitors

Bennett, Robert A. *We'll All Go Home in the Spring: Personal Accounts and Adventures As Told By the Pioneers of the West.* Walla Walla, Wash.: Pioneer Press Books, 1984.

Blaine, David E. *Letters and Papers of Reverend David E. Blaine and His Wife Catharine.* Seattle: Historical Society of the Pacific Northwest Conference of the Methodist Church, 1963.

Brown, Richard Maxwell. "Rainfall and History: Perspectives on the Pacific Northwest." In *Experiences in a Promised Land: Essays in Pacific Northwest History,* ed. G. Thomas Edwards and Carlos A. Schwantes. Seattle: University of Washington Press, 1986.

Cox, Ross. *Adventures on the Columbia River.* New York: J. & J. Harper, 1831.

Denny, Arthur A. *Pioneer Days on Puget Sound.* Seattle: The Alice Harriman Co., 1908.

Gibson, James R. *Farming the Frontier: The Agricultural Opening of the Oregon Country, 1786–1846.* Seattle: University of Washington Press, 1985.

Kane, Paul. *Wanderings of an Artist Among the Indians of North America.* Rutland, Vt.: C. E. Tuttle Co., 1967.

Leighton, Caroline C. *West Coast Journeys, 1865–1879: The Travelogue of a Remarkable Woman.* Seattle: Sasquatch Books, 1995.

Meeker, Ezra. *Pioneer Reminiscences of Puget Sound.* Seattle: Lowman & Hanford, 1905.

Mierzejewski, Steve. "Footprints on the Rivers." Unpublished manuscript, Oregon History Center, Portland, n.d.

Muir, John. *Picturesque California.* New York: J. Dewing, 1988.

Powell, F. W., ed. *Hall J. Kelley on Oregon.* Princeton: Princeton University Press, 1932.

Prosch, Charles. *Reminiscences of Washington Territory: Scenes, Incidents and Reflections of the Pioneer Period on Puget Sound.* Fairfield, Wash.: Ye Galleon Press, 1969.

Swan, James Gilchrist. *The Northwest Coast, or Three Years' Residence in Washington Territory.* New York: Harper & Brothers, 1857.

Victor, Frances Fuller. *All Over Oregon and Washington: Observations on the Country.* San Francisco: John H. Carmany and Co., 1872.

Waring, Guy. *My Pioneer Past.* Boston: Bruce Humphries, 1936.

Whitman, Narcissa. *The Letters of Narcissa Whitman*. Fairfield, Wash.: Ye Galleon Press, 1986.

Winthrop, Theodore. *The Canoe and the Saddle*. New York: J. W. Lovell, 1862.

Forecasting, Local Weather, and Climatic Conditions

Decker, Fred W. *The Weather of Oregon*. Corvallis: Oregon State University, 1960.

Garfielde, Selecius. "Climates of the Northwest." Philadelphia: Ringwalt & Brown, 1872.

Greely, General A. W. *The Climate of Oregon and Washington Territory*. Washington, D.C.: Government Printing Office, 1888.

Lilly, Kenneth E., Jr. *Marine Weather of Western Washington*. Seattle: Starpath, 1983.

Lynott, Bob. *The Weather Tomorrow: Why Can't They Get It Right*. Portland, Ore.: Gadfly Press, 1987.

Pague, B. S. *Second Biennial Report of the Oregon Weather Bureau Cooperating with the United States Department of Agriculture*. 1893.

Renner, Jeff. *Northwest Marine Weather*. Seattle: The Mountaineers Books, 1993.

———. *Northwest Mountain Weather*. Seattle: The Mountaineers Books, 1992.

Rue, Walter. *Weather of the Pacific Coast*. Mercer Island, Wash.: Writing Works, Inc., 1978.

Weber, Erwin L. *In the Zone of Filtered Sunshine: Why the Pacific Northwest Is Destined to Dominate the Commercial World*. Seattle: Pacific Northwest Publishing Co., 1924.

Northwest Fiction, Poetry, and Essays

Davis, H. L. *Honey in the Horn*. New York: Harper & Brothers, 1935.

Dillard, Annie. *The Living*. New York: HarperCollins, 1992.

Doig, Ivan. *Winter Brothers: A Season at the Edge of America*. New York: Harcourt Brace Jovanovich, 1980.

Duncan, David James. *The River Why*. San Francisco: Sierra Club Books, 1983.

Egan, Timothy. *The Good Rain: Across Time and Terrain in the Pacific Northwest*. New York: Alfred A. Knopf, 1990.

Grey, Zane. *The Desert of Wheat*. New York: Harper & Brothers, 1919.

Hugo, Richard. *Making Certain It Goes On: Collected Poems of Richard Hugo*. New York: W. W. Norton, 1984.

———. *A Run of Jacks*. Minneapolis: University of Minnesota Press, 1961.

Jones, Hathaway. *Tall Tales from Rogue River: The Yarns of Hathaway Jones*. Ed. Stephen Dow Beckham. Bloomington: Indiana University, 1979.

Kerouac, Jack. *The Dharma Bums*. New York: Viking Press, 1958.

Kesey, Ken. *Sometimes a Great Notion*. New York: Viking Press, 1964.

MacDonald, Betty. *The Egg and I*. New York: J. B. Lippincott Co., 1945.

McElroy, Colleen J. *Winters Without Snow*. New York: I. Reed Books, 1979.

McKay, Allis. *They Came to a River*. New York: Macmillan, 1941.

Malamud, Bernard. *A New Life*. New York: Farrar, Straus & Cudahy, 1961.

Peterson, Brenda. *Living by Water: Essays on Life, Land and Spirit*. Seattle: Alaska Northwest Books, 1990.

Robbins, Tom. *Another Roadside Attraction*. Garden City, N.Y.: Doubleday, 1971.

———. "Why I Live in Northwestern Washington." In *Edge Walking on the Western Rim: New Works by 12 Northwest Writers,* ed. Mayumi Tsutakawa. Seattle: Sasquatch Books, 1994.

Robinson, Marilynne. *Housekeeping*. New York: Farrar, Straus & Giroux, 1980.

Tisdale, Sallie. *Stepping Westward: The Long Search for Home in the Pacific Northwest*. New York: Henry Holt, 1991.

Anthologies of Northwest Writing

Barcott, Bruce, ed. *Northwest Passages: A Literary Anthology of the Pacific Northwest*. Seattle: Sasquatch Books, 1994.

Holbrook, Stewart, ed. *Promised Land: A Collection of Northwest Writing*. New York: Whittlesey House, 1945.

Ives, Rich, ed. *From Timberline to Tidepool: Contemporary Fiction from the Northwest*. Seattle: Owl Creek Press, 1986.

Lee, W. Storrs, ed. *Washington State: A Literary Chronicle*. New York: Funk & Wagnalls, 1969.

INDEX

A–B

C–D

G—H

I—L

M

N–O

S

W

X–Z

ABOUT THE AUTHOR

David Laskin is the author of *Braving the Elements:
The Stormy History of American Weather* and *A Common Life:
Four Generations of American Literary Friendship and Influence, Eastern
Islands,* and *The Little Girl Book,* among other titles. His articles
have been published in *The New York Times, The Washington Post,
Redbook, Parents,* and the *Seattle Weekly.* He holds an MA in
literature from Oxford and a BA from Harvard and lives
in Seattle with his wife and three daughters.